Thinking Back

Books by C. Vann Woodward

Tom Watson: Agrarian Rebel
Kolombangara and Vella Lavella, 6 August–7 October, 1943
The Bougainville Landing and the Battle of Empress Augusta Bay, 27 October–2 November, 1943
The Battle for Leyte Gulf
Reunion and Reaction: The Compromise of 1877 and the End of Reconstruction
Origins of the New South, 1877–1913
The Strange Career of Jim Crow
The Burden of Southern History
American Counterpoint: Slavery and Racism in the North-South Dialogue
Thinking Back: The Perils of Writing History

Books Edited by C. Vann Woodward

George Fitzhugh, Cannibals All! or, Slaves Without Masters
Lewis H. Blair, A Southern Prophecy: The Prosperity of the South Dependent Upon the Elevation of the Negro
The Comparative Approach to American History
Responses of the Presidents to Charges of Misconduct
Mary Chesnut's Civil War
The Private Mary Chesnut: The Unpublished Civil War Diaries (in collaboration with Elisabeth Muhlenfeld)
The Oxford History of the United States (in progress)

Thinking Back

The Perils of Writing History

C. Vann Woodward

Louisiana State University Press
Baton Rouge and London

Copyright © 1986 by C. Vann Woodward
All rights reserved
Manufactured in the United States of America

Designer: Christopher Wilcox
Typeface: Palatino
Typesetter: Moran Colorgraphic
Printer: Thomson–Shore, Inc.
Binder: John Dekker & Sons, Inc.

Library of Congress Cataloging-in-Publication Data

Woodward, C. Vann (Comer Vann), 1908–
    Thinking back.
    Bibliography: p.
    Includes index.
    1. Woodward, C. Vann (Comer Vann), 1908–
2. Southern States—Historiography.   3. Historians—
United States—Biography.   I. Title.
E175.5.W66A39   1986   975'.0072   85-19692
ISBN 0-8071-1304-2 (cloth)
ISBN 0-8071-1377-8 (paper)

To
the Critics

Without whose devoted efforts
life would have been simpler
but less interesting

Contents

Acknowledgments

T HIS BOOK grew out of an invitation from the Louisiana
State University to deliver the Walter Lynwood Flem-
ing Lectures in Southern History for 1985. The substance of three of the eight chapters was used for that purpose
under the title "Exploring Southern History." The themes of
two chapters were the basis of the Charles Edmonson Historical Lectures I gave at Baylor University the year before. None
of the chapters has appeared in print before, with the exception of Chapter 1, which the *Southern Review* published shortly
before the book appeared in its January, 1986, issue, and parts
of Chapters 4 and 8, which the *New Republic* used in issues of
the same month.

In place of footnote citations I have appended at the back of
the book "A Selective List of Critical Works" that should assist
the reader in locating works mentioned in the text, together
with a few other works of relevant interest. A list of my own
books will be found on the back of the first flyleaf.

I am greatly indebted to Peter Gay, William S. McFeely, Paul

Acknowledgments

M. Gaston, and Susan L. Woodward for reading the manuscript and offering invaluable criticisms and suggestions.
Beverly Jarrett, Associate Director of the Louisiana State University Press, has earned my admiration for the extraordinary
skill and perceptiveness with which she edited this book and
my gratitude for her warmth of personal encouragement and
hospitality.

C. V. W.

New Haven
August, 1985

Thinking Back

History is not truth. Truth is in the telling.

—Robert Penn Warren, "Wind and Gibbon"

. . . you dont love because: you love despite;
not for the virtues, but despite the faults.

—William Faulkner, "Mississippi"

I wol ful fayn at Cristes reverence
Do yow plesaunce leefful, as I kan.
But trusteth wel, I am a southren man.

—Geoffrey Chaucer, "The Parson's Prologue," *Canterbury
Tales*

Prologue

M R. JUSTICE HOLMES, we are told, cherished a quotation from Henrik Ibsen. "Truths," said the playwright, "are by no means the wiry Methuselehs some people think them. A normally constituted truth lives— let us say—as a rule, seventeen or eighteen years; at the outside twenty, seldom longer. And truths so stricken in years are always shockingly thin." Holmes, so far as we know, did not limit the saying to juridical truths, and Ibsen presumably meant for it to apply to other kinds of truth as well, including historical truths.

Historians, perhaps more than some other truth seekers and vendors, may resent ascription of such ephemerality to the truths of their trade, particularly truths of their own devising. As for myself, I do not for a moment accept it in any literal sense. That is not to deny, however, that the older and more experienced historians will in their time have seen enough normally constituted truths come and go, wither and fade, to recognize in Ibsen's pronouncement an element of truth about

3

truths, even the truths of history. Those historians who have worked at their calling long enough to acknowledge responsibility for ideas past the alleged normal life-span will have cause for personal reflections. Those with intellectual progeny of twice the putative life expectancy will have still more cause. And those few who are now answerable for notions going back to the 1930s through three life-spans of verity, down through the 1940s, the 1950s, the 1960s, and 1970s into the 1980s, will have even more reason for sober thought and stocktaking.

That, indeed, is the plight of anyone who began publishing what he put forth as truths, [supposedly new truths](though admittedly nothing is entirely new), as early as the 1930s. There is no disowning or disavowing them, no matter what questionable company they may have fallen into or what hard times may have befallen them. One may defend, deplore, or revise them, but disown them—never. Thin and emaciated though they may have become, there they remain: cited in footnotes, transfixed in textbooks, quoted in monographs with an introductory "although" or "in spite of," distorted perhaps, but undeniably one's own. One misfortune to which they are prone is to become the launching pad for oncoming generations of revisionists. That is one form of what I have called "gerontophagy," the primitive ritual of eating one's elders.

In the discovery and exposure of flaws and fallacies in published works of long standing, a historian may reasonably expect assistance from critics. That expectation has not been disappointed in my particular experience, for critics have been at it early and late—left, right, and center—sometimes at odds with each other as much as with the author, but critical nonetheless. Criticism is the life of the trade in historical ideas and at least half the fun. I have often wondered why others should be permitted to have all the fun when one's own work is the subject and why the author should not claim a share of it by entering into open colloquy with his critics, especially if he is so fortunate—as I have generally been—as to attract the attention of critics who manage to combine candor with civility.

4

Another reason for joining in is that silence may suggest sullen resentment of criticism, or even worse the presumption that the author cherishes the delusion that he has made no mistakes, that he has written the final word. These assumptions may be wholly unjustified, but they are lent credence through persistent silence on the part of the author criticized.

Critics and their views receive a considerable amount of space in the following pages. There are several reasons for this. One is that the subjects I chose to write about have usually been of a controversial nature. I have assumed differences of opinion in choosing them and thus invited and expected criticism. To omit account of it would be to report one side of an ongoing dialogue. Another reason for the attention given to critics herein is that, for better or for worse, my attitude toward them has always been more collegial than adversarial. Granted that criticism involves differences of opinion, so does any worthwhile colleagueship. The adversarial part of the critic's role is certainly present, but it is, or should be, concerned with the discovery of error, in which the author criticized has, or should have, a common interest. And presumably both the critic and the criticized share as their common goal the pursuit of truth. Conceding wryly that this may seem a rather idealized account of the motives involved, I have found that proceeding on that assumption often tends to encourage its adoption by critics, or at least the appearance of it. And that is surely preferable to any contrary assumption about the relationship.

Motives less worthy than the pursuit of truth, including some that are self-serving, are admittedly at work in accounting for the deference and attention to criticism displayed here. On the whole it is better to be criticized than to be ignored or forgotten. Books that go uncriticized are likely to be on the way to superannuation, along with their authors. Aside from criticism that is entirely laudatory or completely devastating, a large category exists that is both provocative and preservative. To consider what the reputations of some historians owe to their critics and to controversy produced and prolonged thereby is to view criticism with a more tolerant and appreciative eye. The example of Frederick Jackson Turner, who died with only two books to his credit, comes to mind. His posthumous publications and the students he inspired no doubt helped, but it is quite clear that there is no explaining Turner's continuing influence without taking into account the vast library of criticism and controversy he provoked. Charles A. Beard was a far more prolific writer than Turner, but his influence was in decline at his death; and like Turner he owed a great deal to continuing criticism—much of it negative, to be sure—for the place his name came to occupy. Other examples could be cited. Like the two mentioned, they would, of course, have produced something worthy of criticism to have stimulated so much of it. Here I am reminded of my colleague in classics, Donald Kagan, who has just completed the third of a four-volume critical work on Thucydides. Few can aspire to such fortunes in fame as these celebrated examples have earned, but their experience might encourage among lesser mortals more tolerance toward criticism.

Running somewhat counter to these impulses of self-exposure is a perverse kind of loyalty to one's intellectual progeny. But it should be the kind of loyalty that does not sour into surly defensiveness or freeze in obstinate refusal to admit error. However frail with age they may have become, however at odds with current fashions, some of these ideas are likely to have acquired over the years a life of their own and to have accumulated followers as well as critics. Since critics, revisionists, and disciples all have a vested interest of some sort in these ideas, they would seem to deserve more than detached bemusement from their progenitor.

One service, explanatory rather than defensive, would be to reconstruct and set forth the circumstances of their conception. To explain need not be to justify or vindicate, but rather to promote understanding and comprehension. It is one of the most common tasks of the historian to fill in the antecedents, the environment, the spirit of the times, the prevailing ideas, prejudices, and patterns of thought surrounding the event he is recounting or explaining. To perform the same function in dealing with historical ideas and interpretations, including one's own, is not to subscribe to the doctrine of historical relativism—the theory that historical interpretations and ideas, even narrative substance, are determined by the environment and interests of the historian. To be explicit, I am not setting up as a historical relativist in this exercise. Nor am I engaged, at least not consciously, in self-vindication and -defense. Rather I see myself as undertaking one of the most familiar functions of the historian—to explain how certain things and ideas came about, and what became of them. Thinking back is, after all, the principal business of historians.

I realize, of course, that this venture is beset by many hazards. It is presumptuous enough for a historian to make his own works the main subject of comment. It is even more presumptuous for him to enter publicly into colloquy about their merits with his critics. It is even worse to try going the critics one better by suggesting criticisms they may have overlooked. In the more reputable circles of the guild this would be regarded as something that is simply "not done." And so far as I know it has not been done. The fact is I cannot think of a suitable precedent for quite this sort of enterprise or I would gladly seek comfort in citing it. There have been numerous autobiographies by historians, to be sure, and a long and reputable tradition supports them. But autobiography this is not. Lacking a precedent, it lacks a name as well. Awareness of isolation in this departure from tradition has caused me misgivings and hesitation about entering upon the venture. Once having overcome those doubts and at least partially thrown off the resulting inhibitions, however, I have found the undertaking less awkward, self-conscious, and embarrassing than expected. At times it has seemed quite natural, even enjoyable—with incidental rewards of catharsis.

It might help to add a word about the title, more particularly the subtitle, chosen for this brief volume. The very briefness

7

of the book suggests a fault commonly found with titles—that they often claim too much. In this instance the "perils" might be thought too numerous and the book too short to cover them. It was my hope that the main title, *Thinking Back*, which suggests personal retrospection (as well, of course, as an occupational commitment), might help to guard against this objection. Further precaution would have entailed stretching the subtitle further by adding the words, "as Illustrated by the Author's Personal Experience." That experience, fortunately enough for me, did not embrace all possible perils the historian is heir to. Nor can it be claimed that those perils I did encounter were necessarily typical, since the writing concerned was largely confined to the history of one century in one region of one country.

Typical or not, the experience likely includes dangers common to many historians, whatever their subject or their period. Other learned professions have faced graver perils. There are theologians, for example, who have been burned at the stake, boiled in oil, and crucified. Historians have not as a rule been subjected to such discomforts. We have furnished few martyrs and fewer saints. It is difficult to imagine a Saint Tacitus or a Saint Gibbon. True, historians have at times been hounded for heresy and banned or pilloried by the state, but usually their perils are subtler. Some of them are self-inflicted by the commission of error, the distortion of evidence, or other offenses against the canons of their own craft for which they bear sole responsibility. Other perils to which they are subject are the work of querulous or uncomprehending critics, headlong revisionists, or careless and prejudiced readers. Then there is the danger cited above in the quotation from Ibsen, that of time's withering effect upon the truths of history and those responsible for them. Of these more common perils the following pages should contain sufficient illustration to justify the title chosen for the book.

8

Chapter 1

Time and Place

T HE TIME was the early 1930s, the place the Southeast-
ern states, the setting the Great Depression. Minor shifts
in time, place, and scene occurred within those years.
In the background of place was growing up in Arkansas and
moving from there to Georgia in 1928. More important, this was
a move from country to city, to Atlanta. Along with that move
came a change of the parental base to Oxford, Georgia, which
served to keep one foot in the soil as well as one in the city.
The next major move was to Chapel Hill in 1934. In the meantime came two summer excursions in Europe, a year of study
at Columbia University in 1931–1932, and two years of teaching at Georgia Tech.

The setting or scene, of course, embraced much more than
the Great Depression, as large as that loomed. For the college
graduate, class of 1930, in the process of discovering his mind
and identity the most exciting scene was intellectual—the high
and most creative years of the Southern Literary Renaissance
in fiction, poetry, and drama. Down underneath that, too low

down to be acknowledged by a young cultural snob, stirred creative explosions in music—the continuous rebirth of jazz. Black in origin, and vulgar as well, jazz was relegated to the unconscious by the proper young white intellectual, but it was part of the scene nevertheless. As was the black world from which it sprang, however misperceived and dimly understood.

Time, place, and scene as well as dramatis personae continued to shift and change as the years passed. But here I am speaking of the formative years, the years when basic commitments are made, goals are set, and the first intellectual progeny are being generated and taking shape. Essentially they are the years when one is being acted upon rather than acting, being shaped rather than shaping. And overwhelmingly, the shaping took place for me in the South and largely by Southern forces, either positive or negative. But it was a South of a particular time, the South of the early 1930s.

What was the South like half a century ago? That is a legitimate, a rather typical, historical question. It could have been asked in 1885, or for that matter in 1785, as well as in 1985. Historians have dutifully squared away with the documentary evidence to answer such questions of earlier periods. I once addressed the question about the 1880s, a half-century later. But here I am speaking not as a historian but as a surviving witness from the period itself. My testimony, therefore, is subject to discount for possessing all the notorious shortcomings of fallible memory and impressionistic evidence. It does claim such merits as a firsthand witness possesses, dubious as they are.

To read about conditions is one thing, to confront them firsthand another. One could read all about the Great Depression at the time and did so daily—the failures, foreclosures, bankruptcies, and shutdowns; the soaring unemployment, the breadlines, the homeless, the hungry, the army of transients, the Hooverville shanty towns, the Dust Bowl. But what did cotton at 4.6 cents a pound and sugar at 3 cents and 25 percent unemployment actually mean in human terms to the millions most affected? One way to find out, a way rarely taken by the college bred, was to go and see.

Maury Maverick was one who tried. "I decided to go out and find what it was all about," he wrote. The flamboyant Texas congressman may not have been a man for all seasons, but he was a man for that season. He tells us:

> I struck out for a real hobo trip. I slept in jungles, got lousy, and what was worse, got preached and lectured at by four-flushing racketeers who called themselves preachers. . . . I saw enough to make anyone sick for a long time. I saw one mother and father sleeping on wet ground, with a baby in between, wrapped in sacks. There was promiscuity, filth, degradation. In some jungles there would be as many as a hundred people in one group. Men and families slept in jails, hot railroad urinals, cellars, dugouts, tumble-down shacks.

That was in the winter of 1932. My most comparable experience came in 1935, a summer job with a New Deal relief agency surveying rural poverty in Georgia. It took me in a car I bought for $30 into the remote backcountry, into Liberty County, Coffee County, Carroll County, to places the news cameras never penetrated, over roads not made for cars. It took me daily into shack after shack and cabin after cabin with my stupid questionnaire forms, face to face with people in conditions that made a mockery of my prescribed questions and embarrassed me for asking them. It was clear that all the misery and hunger and despair had not taken to the road and hobo jungles. Many lacked the strength or the means or the hope ever to leave the entrapment of their rural slums.

The next year, the summer of 1936, James Agee and his collaborator of the camera, Walker Evans, came South. Their sample was in Alabama, as Maverick's had been in Texas and Louisiana and mine in Georgia. They lived with three Alabama families of croppers and tenants, and theirs was a far more intensive experience. Agee was just a year my junior, and

11

it is one of my regrets that I never got to meet him. I saw all that he saw, but it was Agee and Evans who brought it all home to me later in the pit of my stomach by means of their book *Let Us Now Praise Famous Men*. Evans caught their lives with pictures, Agee with words: "shaken with fevers, grieved and made sick with foods, wrung out in work to lassitude in the strong sun and to lack of hope or caring; in ignorance of all cause, all being, all conduct, hope of help or cure, saturated in harm and habit." And on the rare occasions when Agee used their own words he did so with a fine ear: "How did we get caught? Why is it things always seem to go against us? Why is it there can't ever be any pleasure in living? I'm so tired it don't seem like I ever could get rest enough. . . . Sometimes it seems like there wouldn't never be no end to it, nor even a let-up."

Then in 1937—though the pictures were taken in 1935 and 1936—appeared *You Have Seen Their Faces*, the writing by Erskine Caldwell and the camera work by Margaret Bourke-White. The photography was more consciously dramatic and contrived than that of Walker Evans, and Caldwell was the reporter rather than the poet of poverty that Agee was. Her pictures, however, leave no doubt that Bourke-White was in her way capable of portraying the depletion, the defeat, and the humiliation, along with the shame, the bitterness, and the despair of those Alabama faces. Nor did their underlying decency, kindness, and pathetic humility entirely escape her lenses. Here and in Evans' work and Agee's words is an authentic record of human betrayal in the South of a half-century ago.

It was natural that attention should have been focused on rural people of the South, since in 1930 more than two of every three Southerners were rural, 67.9 percent in fact. And 42.8 percent of the region's labor force still worked on farms. Of the industrial work force a large percentage was classified rural, and the majority was less than one generation removed from the farm. Textiles employed more workers than any other single Southern industry. Cotton mills were concentrated along what was, with unconscious irony, called the "Golden Crescent," running along the foothills of the Appalachians in a great curve from North Georgia up through the Carolinas. Chapel Hill was well located as a window on the land of the "lintheads." Back and forth from there to Atlanta in the thirties the pre-throughway roads took me directly along the so-called Golden Crescent, where cotton mills and lintheads were rarely out of sight.

The cotton mill workers, like the workers in other industries, had been the most widely advertised industrial asset of the developing South for fifty years. The New South boosters of the eighties had billed the region's inexhaustible and underemployed labor supply as the most tractable, easily pleased, contented, industrious, and readily available in the whole country. Moreover, they were "of purest Anglo-Saxon stock" and natively averse to unions and strikes. "In the booster rhetoric," as George Tindall put it, "the patient docility of the Saxon churl became almost indistinguishable from that attributed to the African."

Just before the onset of depression, however, the fabled linthead docility suddenly ended with an outburst of strikes, several involving violence. The Golden Crescent was a tinderbox of grievances needing only a spark. The workday was ten to eleven hours long, wages of ten dollars a week were common, living conditions in mill towns were degrading beyond belief, and state labor laws were a century behind the British factory acts. In 1929 a storm of turbulence swept the cotton mills. Strikes were often unorganized and mutinous. Communist-led unions moved into Gastonia, North Carolina, and were met by state militia and mob violence. The labor movement was brutally crushed and the unions left a shambles. When Southern labor stirred next in the 1930s, however, it came to life with the heritage of 1929 militancy supporting it and found sympathy in some universities. At Chapel Hill, mill hand delegations got to know student sympathizers and supporters. By that means the wretchedness of the lintheads became a personal encounter for me about the same time that I encountered the sharecroppers.

The large black component of the Southern scene and the plight of its people at the time seemed to the Southern white youth less of a discovery than the white sharecroppers and mill hands. I had grown up with black people all around, and since they were always there I shared to some extent the common illusion that I was already familiar with them and their problems. What I *was* thoroughly familiar with was one side of the universally prevailing system of racial subordination—the white side and white attitudes. Had my experience been entirely normal, as a twenty-five-year-old youth from Arkansas and Georgia, I would never have known any person of color other than servants and laborers and a few professionals who differed little from them in their demeanor. I would never have had any cause for wonder at the little signs, *White Only* and *Colored*, that appeared everywhere and no reason to question why I had never had a fellow student who was not identifiably white. By 1934, however, this particular youth from the Deep South had already been given reasons to wonder and question, reasons that will be explored later.

These were some of the darker and more forbidding parts of the scene in the early thirties. There were, to be sure, brighter aspects. Among them were the first years of the New Deal and the hopes that it aroused, even though it disappointed many of those hopes later. Still, for a time—for the first time in a long time—one could feel he had a few friends in Washington, friends who might not be very effective but who were doing their best, or seemed to be. Another source of cheer was a growing awareness of the presence of men and women of courage, intelligence, and good will in the South, people who were not blind to the crueler realities of their time and land. They tended to reach out for the like-minded and I soon knew a good many of them. Few were able or willing to speak out. Those who did seemed to me to speak in too mild a voice. The thing was that they lived under powerful inhibitions. These sprang from two sources, one within the South and one originating outside the region.

The inner source had been there a long time, at least since Reconstruction. David Potter was referring to it when he spoke of the "siege mentality" of the South, Howard Odum when he wrote of "a state of mind" that is "manifest in war time," and W. J. Cash in what he called the "savage ideal." It was not a sign or a consequence of unity, but rather of regimentation. Its objective was not so much consensus as conformity. Its methods were not those of persuasion but those of coercion—coercion of the sort that produced the most extreme form of what Tocqueville meant by the "tyranny of public opinion" in America. The coercion took many forms. In its more savage form it resorted to the rope, the lash, and the torch of the mob and the Klan, but it tapered off in milder types of the charivari—or what Southerners called "shivaree"—to hold deviants up to public shame. Those antique and cruder methods were increasingly less necessary as the fundamentalist clergy and the white man's party developed their powerful instruments of regimentation and conformity. Cash summed up the results as well as anyone. "Criticism, analysis, detachment," he wrote, "all those activities and attitudes so necessary to the healthy development of any civilization, every one of them took on the aspect of high and aggravated treason." To doubt or to question the status quo and the received wisdom in any degree was to affront if not insult one's fellow citizens and call in question one's very loyalty.

The outside source of this regimented conformity was an outside as perceived and distorted from the inside, but there can be no doubt of its powerful and conspicuous existence. It took the form of a revival of muckraking, this time confined largely to the Northeast and directed exclusively at the benighted South—the confederacy of rednecks, fundamentalists, demagogues, kluxers, lynchers, boobs, and degenerates. Combining a literature of exposure with one of satire and rid-

15

icule, South-baiting became a Northern journalistic industry with fabulously rich resources to mine below the Potomac. Among favored subjects were lynching, peonage, chain gangs, convict labor, child labor, mill towns, sharecropping, corrupt courts and politics, illiteracy, laziness, poverty, bigotry, hookworm, pellagra.

All these evils existed, of course, however often denied or minimized. But what outraged the besieged beyond endurance was the contempt, the jeering, and the ridicule that often accompanied their exposure. The supreme master of ridicule was H. L. Mencken, and it did not help that his headquarters were below the Mason and Dixon line in Baltimore. None of his many imitators could match the master. The South, he declared, was the "bunghole of the United States, a cesspool of Baptists, a miasma of Methodism, snake-charmers, phoney real-estate operations, and syphilitic evangelists." Mencken probably reached his peak in the late 1920s, as did the South-baiting industry in general. But its influence and productivity persisted into the 1930s and spread through the academy, especially among the social scientists. Investigators of Southern atrocities and monstrosities poured through from the North.

Even if a Southerner mustered the courage to overcome the inner restraints of the siege mentality and its coercions, there remained the chorus of jeers and taunts from extramural sources to contend with. The siege mentality resulted in part, at least, from being besieged. To make common cause with the Yankee South-baiters in order to attack the brutalities and stupidities of the intramural police was to raise troubling inner doubts about one's own deeper loyalties. Those eager allies from outside did not invariably harbor the most disinterested of motives. If to embrace them and their missions were to endorse and align oneself with their self-righteousness and venomous sneers, this would surely not cast one in the most congenial company. Yankee scorn of the South was an old story, but added to scorn was now ridicule and contempt. It was one thing for the college boy to rush for the most recent issue of the

American Mercury to be the first to quote Mencken's latest quip about "the miasmatic jungles" of darkest Arkansas. It was quite another for a budding scholar from that state to place himself on the outset of his career beyond the tolerance or even the endurance of his native region. Other allies and another environment were indicated.

Chapel Hill then enjoyed the reputation of being an oasis in the Sahara of the Bozart. By 1934, however, the depression had dried up or slowed down the flow of its wellsprings. Money was tight, and administrators were increasingly cautious in the face of a critical legislature and a suspicious public. Even in its heyday Chapel Hill had never dared seriously to challenge prevailing Southern racial proscriptions and orthodoxies. There were, of course, no black students or faculty and no acknowledgment of their ethnic interests and regional contributions in the curriculum. A few radical white students, largely of New York or metropolitan origin, were tolerated and made their presence felt. And the university commitment to freedom of speech was strong enough to protect most, though not all, of the usual assortment of visiting spokesmen for causes and ideas.

The foundation of Chapel Hill's reputation for freedom and innovation, however, lay in the arts, the performing and writing arts, and especially play writing and staging. Paul Green was then in his prime as a prize-winning playwright. The shadow of Thomas Wolfe lingered about, and the novelist himself turned up for a visit. William T. Couch, still in his early thirties, presided over the University of North Carolina Press, which was then the most active and influential publishing house in the South. He hospitably entertained a stream of writers and aspiring authors, many of whom I met at his home.

On the fringes of this activity existed a small community of provincial bohemians or would-be bohemians, partly but not wholly outsiders and regarded with some askance by insiders. Not long after I arrived on the scene I was called into the office of Howard Odum, to whom I owed my fellowship at the university, and confronted with the question of how it was I could have managed to be there only three weeks and already to have fallen in with the "wrong crowd." The hang-out of the wrong crowd was Abernethy's Book Store, just across Franklin Street from the main campus. It was there that the manifestoes were composed and the new books thumbed through before sale, and it was there that *Contempo*, a now-long-extinct periodical of advanced views was edited. Since that publication was probably the only thing Gertrude Stein knew about Chapel Hill when she came to speak at the university, it was to the book shop she headed when she arrived. I happened to be temporarily in charge of the till when she walked in and was struck quite speechless with the wonder of it all. Despite professorial admonition, my attachment to the wrong crowd persisted.

Chapel Hill was a sort of intellectual crossroads of the South in those years. Roads led in and out and crisscrossed. There was a Chapel Hill–Atlanta–New South liberal axis, and a much dimmer Chapel Hill–New York–Union Square radical axis. Meanwhile a Nashville–Baton Rouge–Old South Agrarian axis was shaping up, taking form eventually in the *Southern Review*. Between those axes ran the embattled road from Chapel Hill to Nashville that was alleged—with exaggeration—to be bristling with hostilities and practically impassable: Vanderbilt Agrarians *vs.* Tar Heel Liberals.

Personal encounters between the two camps were rare, but in 1936 there occurred a dramatic confrontation in the form of a debate at Nashville. Accompanying W. T. Couch, who defended the Chapel Hill cause singlehandedly, I was an apprehensive witness to the event. Couch had his hands full, since the front row was filled with Agrarians, authors of *I'll Take My Stand*, and several of them joined in the attack. Voices and tempers rose to a high pitch, and the exchange ended suddenly with the dramatic withdrawal of the Agrarians led by Allen Tate. They filed from the front row up the center aisle and out the door, with Tate shouting final imprecations. At a bar later I fell into conversation with an unidentified man who turned out to be Andrew Lytle, the novelist. He insisted that we continue our talk and drinks at an informal gathering where he was sure I would be most welcome. The gathering proved to be that of the Agrarians, who were celebrating their triumph over poor Couch. Some embarrassment followed my identification as a friend of the foe, but good manners prevailed and despite some awkwardness the door was opened to some relationships of lasting importance and meaning to me.

Presiding over the traffic at North Carolina in the 1930s was the benign spirit of Frank Graham. For the first of my three years at the university I occupied a rented room in a house directly behind President Graham's official residence on Franklin Street. This made casual personal encounters natural and not infrequent and helped turn an attitude of respect into one of affection. The man was all but irresistible. It is impossible here to assess or so much as suggest his significance for the South of that time, but it is necessary to mention one of Frank Graham's contributions. That was to serve, however cautiously and reluctantly, first as intermediary and eventually, when he became president of the Southern Conference for Human Welfare in 1938, as avuncular sponsor for the left wing of Southern New Dealers.

All things considered—including the alternatives among more-celebrated universities—Chapel Hill was not a bad place for a young Southerner in his midtwenties to be in the mid-1930s. Especially one who was facing so many crossroads of his own life and career at that particular time. How could I reconcile being a Southerner with so many impulses then considered anti-Southern? Convictions and loyalties collided constantly. Underlying tensions had to be worked out—tensions between the modern and the traditional, the cosmopolitan and the provincial, between radical and conservative, rebellion and compromise. One might harbor both literary and scholarly impulses, and my immediate circle, both at Chapel Hill and at Emory, shared more of the former than the latter. I had friends who were Agrarians and friends who were Marxists. Some were even Liberals, a term not yet opprobrious. How was one to come to terms with all these incongruities?

Whatever the extracurricular experience at Chapel Hill contributed to sorting out, resolving, or complicating these problems—and it undoubtedly did contribute—that contribution was largely unanticipated. It seemed at the time incidental to the declared purpose of earning scholarly credentials. Yet the ostensible purpose was incidental to undeclared expediencies. The fact was that the commitment to degree-earning was prompted by a prior commitment to finishing a book begun the year before my arrival at the university and with no thought of becoming a professional historian. After a year of research and the writing of some four chapters of a biography of Tom Watson, I had run out of money. The best hope of completing the book seemed to lie in getting a fellowship for graduate work in history and offering the book as a dissertation. And the logical university for the purpose seemed to be North Carolina, since its library held the voluminous private papers of the man whose biography I was writing.

The matter of the needed stipend had already been attended to by Howard W. Odum, who happened in the summer of 1934 to be paying a visit to his parents, a mile down the road toward Covington from my parents' home in Oxford, Georgia. Informed of my purpose in calling on him, he took me immediately to the barn where he was weaning a calf and instructed me pointedly on the procedure while hearing about my lofty intellectual aspirations. It was a thoroughly Odum-esque performance—down to earth. My case for the stipend was undoubtedly furthered by a word from Odum's protégé and colleague in sociology at North Carolina, Rupert B. Vance. That connection came of another parental coincidence: his parents had been neighbors of mine in Morrilton, Arkansas, and I had worked for his father there one summer as a hired hand.

The Odum-Vance team headed the most thriving academic empire in the South at that time. Odum's close links with the private foundations and his cautious diplomacy tided his enterprise over the shoals of depression and floated his school of regional sociology handsomely. The two men, but especially Vance, were initially my closest personal ties at the university. But their field was sociology, and I had tried that discipline for two full and shattering days as a graduate student at Columbia in 1931 before transferring to political science in desperation to acquire an M.A. Anyway, my writing commitment in 1934, though begun independent of previous brushes with the academy and with no academic purpose in mind, pointed irrevocably to history. In that department I therefore registered, endowed as I was with nothing but the faintest formal preparation on the American side. One dull term's course as an undergraduate at Emory University (in which I sat beside David Potter) had been more than enough to discourage further curiosity.

With a fresh if empty mind and an exciting book of my own underway, I reasoned that perhaps I would now see this unexplored field take on a new glamor and I would rise to the challenge. Much better minds had done so. After all, I was nearly four years older since my first brush with the subject and far riper in wisdom—or so I thought. The first thing to do, I was told, was to master the standard "sets"—the old *American Nation* series, the *Yale Chronicles*, and others guaranteed to bring one up to date. Noting with some puzzlement that most of the many volumes were already a generation old, I nevertheless plunged in. That first plunge was chilling. Plodding through volume after volume, I began to wonder if I had ever encountered prose so pedestrian, pages so dull, chapters so devoid of ideas, whole volumes so wrongheaded or so lacking in point. Was there anything memorable about what one was expected to remember? Was this the best my newly chosen profession could do? Was it what I would be expected to do? A career, a lifetime dedicated to inflicting such reading on innocent youth? Or accepting it as a model for myself? Fleeing the stacks repeatedly, I spent much of that first year pacing Franklin Street by night debating whether I might fare better as a fruit-peddler, panhandler, or hack-writer.

A few rays of hope eventually broke through. A seminar in second-century Roman history served as a reminder that history could be absorbing and that Gibbon had written some of it. A few intensive encounters with American documents in pursuit of a thesis stirred the sporting blood and the spirit of the hunt. Research evidently could be fun. The gradual discovery of works on American history of genuine merit, as well as the discovery of a few kindred spirits who shared the dilemmas of apprenticeship inspired hope. Perhaps it might be possible, after all, to make one's peace and find satisfaction in the strange guild to which by coincidence I found myself joined.

Hardest of all to accept was the predominant literature, the scholarship, and the prevailing interpretations in my own field of Southern history. I mean by "my own," the field into which I was inescapably thrust by coincidence, by chance, but primarily by prior commitment to a dissertation subject. However fascinating it might be, Roman history would never do as a major field for a candidate who insisted upon presenting to the faculty his study of a provincial popular leader of the nineteenth-century South. A Southern historian I must be—or somehow become—whatever my growing antipathy to the work of my predecessors in the field.

To explain so strong an aversion to the existing corpus of historical scholarship to which I proposed to contribute it would not be enough to give a detached appraisal of Southern historiography. At the risk of some unfairness and distortion, it would be more to the point to view it through the eyes of the young novice concerned, whatever his limitations and biases. To me at the time each of the masters held up as models for emulation seemed virtually of one mind, united not so much in their view of the past as in their dedication to the present order, the system founded on the ruins of Reconstruction called the New South. That system, already in its sixth decade, still had two more decades to go (as it turned out). It faced the future with pride and confidence and an unstinting faith in its founders and their precepts. This faith and pride seemed as fully shared by historians of the antebellum South as by those of more recent periods. In many and varied ways the histories they wrote joined in vindicating, justifying, rationalizing, and often celebrating the present order. Sharing neither their faith nor their pride in that order, I naturally questioned their histories. Both the critic and the criticized, be it admitted, were responding primarily to the present rather than to the past.

The "present" for me, the intellectual present in which I came of age, was the peak and crest of the Southern Literary Renaissance. No Southern youth of any sensitivity could help being excited by the explosion of creativity taking place during the early 1930s—in fiction, in poetry, in drama. Nor could I help seeing that the novelists, poets, and playwrights were in the main writing about the same South historians were writing about and making the whole world of letters at home and abroad read what they wrote and ring with their praise. With this awareness and the expectations it aroused, I arrived as a young apprentice at the doors of the history guild for training—and what a striking contrast, what a letdown, what a falling off! No renaissance here, no surge of innovation and creativity, no rebirth of energy, no compelling new vision. This was a craft devoted primarily at the time, or so it seemed to me, to summing up, confirming, illustrating, and consolidating the received wisdom, the regional consensus that prevailed uniquely in the South of the 1930s and—though I could not then have known it—was to continue through the 1940s. That consensus proclaimed the enduring and fundamentally unbroken unity, solidarity, and continuity of Southern history.

The most celebrated Southern historian of the time was Ulrich B. Phillips of Yale, foremost authority on the history of slavery and the plantation. As perceived from Carolina, he seemed to embody New South more than Old South values, to preach the continuity of New South with Old, to see the old order as anticipating and preparing the way for the new. Not only was slavery a school for civilizing Africans, but the plantation was an efficient training camp for future captains of industry. The planters' efficiency and skills in labor management were models for the industrializing of the New South and their example proved the necessity for white supremacy.

Over the history of the Confederacy and the Civil War loomed the towering reputation of Douglas Southall Freeman, whose four-volume *R. E. Lee* appeared in 1934. In that work and volumes that followed, Freeman not only glorified a flawless hero for the postwar South, but justified the Lost Cause as well. W. B. Hesseltine, in *Confederate Leaders in the New South*, was to draw the moral later that "one by one, the Southern states were 'redeemed' by their old leaders," that it was by his "full acceptance of the new social order" that "Lee became the embodiment of the spirit of the New South" determined "to build a new society on a Northern model." The new order, therefore, not only had the blessings of the old, it was continuous with it and led by Old South leaders.

Reconstruction history had no presiding genius of the stature of Phillips or Freeman. Loosely attributed to the Dunning school, the prevailing and all but universally received interpretation preceded Dunning and was more the product of a regional white consensus than of a school or a scholar. The authority of the academy stood behind the consensus, however, and scholars contributed abundantly to it. Aspiring revisionists were warned by E. Merton Coulter, for example, against any "departure from the well-known facts." The well-known facts constituted the perfect justification for the discrediting of Reconstruction, its overthrow by almost any means required, its replacement by the Redeemers, and the legitimizing of their regime. A few scholars had questioned the orthodox picture— R. H. Woody and Francis B. Simkins in a study of South Carolina and W. E. B. Du Bois in *Black Reconstruction*, for example—but they had little effect. In the academy and out, in North as well as South, was stamped the tragic image of a betrayed,

savaged, and humiliated people and a South degraded beyond endurance by the corrupt rule of carpetbaggers, blacks,
and scalawags. Rarely has history served a regime better by
discrediting so thoroughly the old order from which the new
rulers seized power.

The history of the New South regime itself, after the seizure
of power, was first written by enthusiastic proponents and advocates of the New South crusade, or lifted directly from their
promotional literature and indistinguishable from it. Philip
Alexander Bruce of Virginia led off with a huge volume entitled *The Rise of the New South* (1905), which told how the Southern states had "risen from the dust of absolute ruin" to a
"greater prosperity" than that of the antebellum order. By their
"courage and wisdom" they had made this "the most honor-
able period in their history," "one of the noblest chapters in
the annals of our country," one that would be "unsurpassed,
pehaps unequalled in the record of any other part of the
Union." One secret of success by the ruling elements of "intelligence and property" was their program of disfranchisement that had struck a blow at "the principle of manhood suffrage . . . a blow that ultimately will completely destroy it." The
new laws, he said, "will eliminate with equal effectiveness the
least intelligent and the least conservative elements among the
white and black voters alike."

When academic historians got around to the period, their
contributions modified the rhetoric of approbation only
slightly. Holland Thompson, the first of them, in *The New South*
(1919) faithfully echoed the tone of cheerful optimism, confidence, and pride in the triumphs and prospects of the new order. A more interesting example of academic New South history was a learned monograph from Johns Hopkins, Broadus
Mitchell's *The Rise of Cotton Mills in the South* (1921). Although
he called himself a Marxist and once ran for office on the Socialist ticket, Mitchell grew up in South Carolina and Virginia
with a father to whom the son confesses he owed his point of
view, that of the New South gospel. He undertook, he says,

"not only an industrial chronicle, but a romance, a drama as well." The romance was that of Southern industrialization, led in its initial stages by the old planter aristocrats in a New South that received from the Old South the heritage of "an ingrained and living social morality"—noblesse oblige, paternalism, philanthropy and all—more continuity of the Phillipsian school.

One minor challenge of historians to the New South consensus deserves mention, that of Benjamin B. Kendrick and Alex M. Arnett, *The South Looks at Its Past* (1935). They dared question the part of the doctrine that stressed white unity, continuity, and sectional reconciliation by pointing to evidence of sharp conflict not only intersectional but intrasectional as well. Another challenge came in the form of a polemical tract from Texas, W. P. Webb's *Divided We Stand* (1937). These dissents, however, were completely overshadowed by the arrival of support for the New South interpretation from Harvard in a celebrated 1937 book by Paul H. Buck, *The Road to Reunion, 1865–1900*. A history of reconciliation between North and South, Buck's study enriched our understanding of the problems and rituals of reunion. Since he regarded the restoration of "a sense of nationality . . . based upon consciousness of national strength and unity" as the noblest achievement of the period, however, he tended to applaud whatever contributed to that end. The New South gospel of reconciliation appealed to him strongly. Granted certain imperfections in the system, he wrote, those with "a more realistic conception of conditions in the South took a more cheerful attitude." Perhaps the imperfections, especially when one considered "the easy and even indolent adaptation of the mass of Negroes," were a small price to pay for peace and reunion. After all, the Radicals were "only the sickest of the nerve-shot age," and the Negro had by now "discarded the foggy notions of Reconstruction."

Such were my despairing perceptions of the received wisdom about the South's past that prevailed around 1937—and was to prevail for some years to come, on through the next decade. These impressions were admittedly crude and immature at the time. And yet, thinking back from a much later and presumably more mature perspective, I confess that I find in those youthful impressions much that still holds up. A consensus did prevail among historians in the 1930s, a uniquely broad consensus that papered over the breaks and fissures and conflicts in Southern history with myths of solidarity and continuity. Only with the support of such a consensus could a writer like Wilbur J. Cash have undertaken a book about "*the* mind" of the whole region from past to present and gained wide acclaim and credence for his efforts.

Any challenge of revision to such a broadly based consensus would be a formidable, perhaps foolhardy undertaking, especially if it started with a rejection of most of the underlying assumptions on which the consensus was based. But then, youth is the time for foolhardy ventures.

Chapter 2

Biography and the Biographer

TO ATTACK the ramparts of the establishment in Southern historiography head-on would obviously have been unwise. Especially so when its views commanded such universal popular support as they did in the 1930s. Even a fledgling could see that. Even with credentials in hand, I understood that the attack would have to be oblique and could only be launched with any promise of effectiveness from outling works of my own construction.

What was needed was a subject in Southern history and a means of writing it that would expose what seemed to be the fallacies, omissions, and long silences that characterized the New South school. These included the persistent themes of continuity and unity, particularly the continuity of the new order with the old and the unity of all whites through history. Along with these went "the Central Theme" of white supremacy, the denial or neglect of conflict between the classes, races, and sections, and the choral accompaniment of progress and prosperity, political conservatism, and sectional reconciliation.

To confess such objectives is to risk giving two misleading impressions. First, if it suggests the fulfillment of long-term professional objectives, I should remind the reader that I was not even aware of the presumed errors of Southern historians that I now set out to correct before encountering them quite recently in graduate school, and that I had already selected my subject with other objectives in mind. Secondly, the confessed objective of subversive revision might invite the serious indictment of writing "history with a purpose." If the implied alternatives be writing history without a purpose or with unacknowledged or unconscious purpose, then the indictment will have to stand. Such defenses as occurred to me at the time were later put forth by H. Stuart Hughes, who expressed better than I ever did what I had long felt. "Unless there is some emotional tie," he wrote, "some elective affinity linking the student to his subject, the results will be pedantic and perfunctory." And furthermore, "The man who does not feel issues deeply cannot write great history about them." Even earlier, Walter Webb, admitting that *The Great Plains* was written "in a state of suppressed emotion," declared himself "utterly shameless" on that point, "because I believe that deep feeling for a subject makes for harder work and better writing." Peter Gay gives eloquent expression to this view in his *Style in History*. Admittedly there were dangers in this precept, for strong feelings can produce bad history as well as good. But I took what comfort I could from such thoughts.

For the purposes outlined above, the subject to which I was already committed, a biography of the Georgia Populist Thomas E. Watson seemed made to order in many respects. The deeper I got into the story of Watson's tempestuous career through Southern history from Reconstruction to the Great War, the more possibilities of this sort I perceived. Not only was it a fascinating story in itself, but it plunged the historian into all the dark, neglected, and forbidden corners of Southern life shunned by the New South school. At the same time it compelled reconsideration of all the cheerful aspects on which that school preferred to dwell: progress, prosperity, peace, consensus, white solidarity, black contentment, sectional reconciliation, and the overarching themes of unity, continuity, and nationalism. No realistic study of Watson could leave any of these shibboleths unchallenged.

First of all, Tom Watson brought to front and center the Populist upheaval and its impact on the South. Populism had in its time won support from very few Southern intellectuals and nothing but scorn and ridicule from the dominant class. Furthermore the agrarian revolt, especially in its third-party phase, was an embarrassment to many New South doctrines and a contradiction of the favorite themes of the historians, especially those of white solidarity and black contentment. Consequently the Populist movement was generally shunted aside, minimized, or silently passed over. To give it rightful attention would be to emphasize conflict rather than consensus and to play up poverty, injustice, and conflict rather than recovery, prosperity, and peace. It was little wonder that Populism was simply not considered a very respectable subject for historians—not when the Old South, the Civil War, and Reconstruction were available as subjects.

Other risks to orthodox views arose from focusing on the agrarian rebellion and its spokesmen. To give them the floor and hear them out on Henry Grady and his allies and their policies, propaganda, and politics of the 1880s was to expose the New South in its making in all its crass and materialistic essentials. These included class favoritism, subservience to wealth, and indifference to growing impoverishment of the countryside. Disrespectful Populist critics also exposed the hypocrisy of disguising the new order in the garments of the Old South and parading Confederate worthies as figureheads of state and industry. The New South double-think of worshiping the symbols and myths of the Lost Cause and simultaneously serving the masters of the new plutocracy was too much for Populist critics. So was the reverence and deference demanded for the Redeemers, the South's new rulers who overthrew and succeeded the Reconstruction regime. The Populists had taken the measure of the justice and probity dispensed by the Redeemers. Most concretely they had seen their methods displayed in the numerous elections of which they had been robbed by blatant fraud, terror, and force. To take full account of the Populist experience promised to open the way to extensive revision of accepted views of the New South, or at least to suggest the need for revisions.

The first question was how could such elaborate historical revisions, even a beginning of them, be legitimately hung upon a biography, especially the biography of a man with such a reputation as Tom Watson's. The memory of him was still fresh in many minds, for he had only been dead since 1922. It was natural that the surviving popular image of the man was shaped mainly by his last years. During those last ten or twelve of his more than sixty-six years Watson had earned and probably deserved the name of the very prototype of the Southern demagogue, the type at its fullest flowering. His name in that phase of his life was unquestionably associated with mob violence, lynching, Ku Kluxery, vicious racism directed at both blacks and Jews, anti-Catholicism, and red-baiting—all in extreme form—culminating in his political rejuvenation and a seat in the United States Senate. How could such a man be taken seriously as the symbol of anything but the worst? Indeed, how could one make sense of him at all?

That was the essential problem for Watson's biographer. As biographical puzzles go, I can think of few more baffling. Was it possible to make credible and understandable to readers with good reason for skepticism a figure who combined in one lifetime so many contradictions, who was both admirable and despicable? For I felt justified, indeed impelled by the evidence, to present Watson in his earlier years as a leader of unusual courage, intelligence, and integrity, a man who fearlessly defied some of the most powerful and ruthless forces of his time, who repeatedly exposed himself to danger and threats to his life, and who proved for a time capable of incorruptible devotion to a cause he deeply believed in and one I felt deserved a sympathetic hearing.

For the biographer there was at least one brighter side to all this. At least I would be spared the temptation to which biographers too often yield, that of becoming apologists for their subject, or even ignoring faults and inconsistencies and endowing him with consistently noble attributes and qualities. There had been a previous biography of Watson, the work of William W. Brewton, a sincere and devoted follower who reconciled the contradictions by endowing his subject with integrity and consistency from beginning to bitter end. I knew from the start that this option was not open to me. In fact I had been drawn to the subject initially by what I then perceived to be an unparalleled opportunity to expose all that was worst in Southern life and politics. In other words I began with a commitment to the prevailing image of Tom Watson, the one so well grounded on the last years of his career. It was only later that the full complexities of the undertaking began to dawn upon me.

To acknowledge and record the inconsistencies and contradictions, however faithfully and fully, is not to fulfill all of the functions of a biographer. It is also reasonable to expect him to venture some explanatory theory, or some narrative framework in the telling that would make sense of wild discrepancies, that would make one man out of two personalities so much at odds with each other. There was, however, no black magic available to explain the Dr. Jekyll–and–Mr. Hyde problem I faced. Unlike Robert Louis Stevenson's fiction, the Jekyll and Hyde of my subject did not appear alternatively, early and late, nor was the transformation instantaneous or recurrent. The Jekyll in Tom Watson was clearly predominant well into his middle years, and the Hyde in him did not take overwhelming possession until the last fifteen years of his life. Between the two contrasting periods was a gray decade or so of transition, from about 1896 to 1908, when the two personalities contended for possession, with the Hyde contender increasingly gaining the upper hand over the Jekyll.

Acknowledging to myself that I had no pat psychological theory, no comprehensive explanation of the enigma that I could spell out with conviction, I adopted the strategy of sharing what clues I had and relying on the narrative line and its logical requirements to provide the reader with all available evidence to form his own theory. That strategy of mine has been considered an evasion of the biographer's duty. I prefer to think of it as a deferential sidestepping. At least I withheld no contrary evidence in the Dr. Jekyll or the Mr. Hyde part of the story. On an assumption no more sophisticated than the old one that the child is father to the man, I stressed an "unusually quick temper and a disposition to attack with waspish fury on small provocation" in his boyhood. Along with this were instances described as "peevish irascibility," "tyrannical petulance," and "sheer red rage"—including his demolishing a buzzing circular saw with a sledge hammer during a quarrel with his brother. Such outbursts recall the terrible passions in which Thomas Jefferson witnessed the youthful Andrew Jackson "choke with rage."

More revealing of the darker side of my youthful Jekyll was a remarkable letter Watson at the age of twenty-six wrote his wife. In it he complained of being reared by "fitful harshness" instead of being "firmly governed" by his parents, and of being "abused, ridiculed, mocked and scorned." This, he believed, had "poisoned"his life. "I have imagined enemies where there were none: been tortured by indignities which were the creatures of my own fancy, and have magnified the gloom of every reverse." Commenting on this, I pointed out as "perhaps a clue for the psychologist" that in his autobiographical novel, *Bethany: A Story of the Old South* (1904), Watson "speaks of his mother with a passionate devotion," makes himself several years older than he was, and has his father die when the son was a baby.

On the whole, the biography, when it was published in 1938, enjoyed a most generous reception. But there have been later criticisms. One of them charges a failure to exploit or intelligently use psychological analysis and insights. This stricture may well be justified. It was questioned, however, by the psychiatrist Robert Coles, who found the psychological problems of the Watson biography quite satisfactorily handled. My old friend David Potter went so far as to single out the psychological aspect of the book for special praise.

On the other hand a more recent critic, Barton C. Shaw, takes issue with the Jekyll-and-Hyde contrast, contending that "no drastic transformation in Watson's nature took place" and that he had always been "a profoundly troubled individual." This seems to me to risk turning upside down the solution of the earlier biographer, the admirer of Watson, who also denied any drastic change but found his hero consistently admirable from beginning to the end. Any future attempt to impose consistency and continuity on an interpretation of Tom Watson's life will face awkward contradiction from the evidence.

Granted that the seeds of personality flaws and defects are implanted quite early in life, and may always be latently present, their manifestations in behavior can take many and wildly contrasting forms. Yet there were not two Tom Watsons, but one. The Watson who picked fights with childhood playmates, college classmates, and fellow lawyers, who insulted Populist associates, and even attacked a circular saw was the Watson who later set howling mobs in action against Negroes, Catholics, Socialists, and Jews and who drove crazed killers to bloody deeds. But the differences between the outbursts of the earlier and the later period are important, and they lie not only in the objects of his wrath, the injustice of and motives for his attacks, and the appalling social consequences of his deeds, but also in the startling escalation of pathological irrationality in the man himself. In 1915 he wrote a medical friend, seeking professional advice about "a baffling nervous trouble" that periodically rendered him "so despondent and distressed, *about nothing,* that it is difficult to live." In the biography I did not use the Jekyll-and-Hyde metaphor, but relied on the evidence to establish the contradictory elements of his personality. The evidence of the contrast seemed much more abundant and clear than that for any explanation I might put forth. I felt constrained to rest my case on the evidence.

The most controversial aspect of the benevolent Jekyll side of the portrait was my treatment of Watson's policy toward race relations and the Negro. On this I went so far as to say that "Tom Watson was perhaps the first native white Southern leader of importance to treat the Negro's aspirations with the seriousness that human strivings deserve" and that "never before or since have the two races in the South come so close together" as under his leadership of the Populists. Even further, I said that in years when racial violence was at its peak, and Georgia led the country in lynchings, Watson "faced his problem courageously, honestly, and intelligently," and "met each issue squarely." He vowed to "make lynch law odious to the people," to prove that "the accident of color can make no difference in the interests of farmers, croppers, and laborers," and to assure black people their full political and legal rights and participation in his party.

Critics have scored several telling points, mainly since the 1960s, against this flattering picture of Watson's racial attitudes and policies. They have rightly cited evidence of underlying paternalism, racism, and condescension in his attitudes toward blacks and signs that as early as 1895 he began to withdraw from his advanced position on Negro rights. I am persuaded by these and other criticisms that I was incautious and went too far in this matter and that my critics were justified in calling me to terms. In a later book I acknowledged that Populist gains in interracial cooperation "were limited and that their significance is easily exaggerated."

With regard to this failing, I call attention to two circumstances, not for the purpose of excusing error, but rather to explain it. The first is the perspective from which the book was

written, that of the 1930s, when blacks had long been thoroughly disfranchised and depoliticized and no white Southern politician dared speak out for their political or civil rights.
In writing about a Southern politician who *had* dared speak out
in the 1890s, when violence and danger were much greater, it
was perhaps more understandable that I should have stressed
the comparative boldness and success of Watson's efforts rather
than their limitations and shortcomings. Furthermore, though
the underlying racism and paternalism were undoubtedly
there, they had taken on after the 1960s an altered significance.

The second circumstance was internal to the biography and
its author. In quoting Watson as determined to "make lynch
law odious to the people," for example, I knew that I would
eventually be quoting the same man as saying twenty years
later that *"lynch law is a good sign: it shows that a sense of justice
yet lives among the people"* and that he would no more hesitate
to lynch a Negro "rapist" than to shoot a mad dog. The striking contrast between the early and the late pronouncements
on lynching surely accounts for the emphasis on the former.
Nuances of complexity in history can apply not only to changes
in the times, but to changes in individuals as well. None of
which justifies errors in the writing of history or biography, but
it might assist in explaining why and how they are made.

There is history in every biography, or should be, and it is
subject to the same hazards of error. To anticipate one of them,
in writing in the 1930s about the strivings and troubles of the
Populists in the 1890s, I could not help being influenced by
analogies between their times and my own, by the similarities
between the depression in which they struggled and the one
in which we were then still floundering. These comparisons
could be treacherous, of course, but they could also be illuminating, and they cetainly lent zest to the enterprise. It was
no dead past I was trying to bring to life, but one very much
alive and full of meaning. The hazards lay in overplaying similarities and overlooking differences, in permitting sympa-

thies to betray one into partisanship, and in linking present motives with past policies. I am sure I might have been better warned and more conscious of such traps than I was at the outset.

I do not wish to suggest that I was a pioneer in the history of Southern Populism. John D. Hicks had already published his general study, *The Populist Revolt*, which included treatment of the South. Alex M. Arnett had come forth with a study of Georgia Populists before Hicks, and there were monographs on two other Southern states. All of these, and especially Arnett, were helpful, but I believed that I had something to add, some new ways of viewing the movement. Several approaches and ideologies to which I had been exposed competed for dominance in my own interpretation. Prominent among them were those of the Agrarians, the Marxists, the Liberals, and ideas associated with the name of Charles Beard. For all the diversity and divergence separating them, each school retained some appeal, though at the same time all presented enough obstacles to inhibit full commitment to any one of them. At the risk of being taken for a hopeless eclectic, however, I would admit that all these diverse schools left some mark.

If pressed to say which influence was the most discernible I suppose I should have to say that of Beard, though with alterations and reservations I will later point out. That would not be attributable to his writings alone, however, but also to the influence of my mentor, Howard K. Beale, who anticipated much of the interpretation of the Civil War in Charles and Mary Beard's *The Rise of American Civilization*. I did not accept all of either, but this is an opportunity I must take to acknowledge a debt to Howard Beale as a scrupulous, exacting, and intelligent critic of the written word. Without his criticism there would have been a much wider gap in quality and in time between dissertation and published book. With it there was no gap at all save the time normally required for printing, since a carbon of the former served as copy for the latter.

My treatment of Populism was clearly sympathetic, and some would later say partisan. Populism did eventually take the form of a third party, but its earlier history and origins as a popular movement and ideology lay in the Farmers Alliance several years earlier. What seemed to deserve emphasis was the spirited way in which masses of people bred to a traditionalist culture and deference to their "betters," after being sunk for decades in poverty and defeatism, suddenly roused themselves from torpor and apathy and mounted a rebellion. They defied their betters in banks, railroads, industry, business, and political office as their oppressors. They ridiculed the editorial pap from the businessman's press and the New South celebrators. They rejected white solidarity, ridiculed their old party as identical with the other, and organized their own. They embraced as allies industrial labor and blacks as well, then spoke out for the rights of both. In the process the Populists put together one of the earliest and most thoroughgoing critiques of corporate America and its culture we have had. In accounting for the defeat and collapse of their party I stressed the fraud, violence, and chicanery used against them in elections by the old party.

Much scholarship has gone into the history of Populism since the 1930s, and some of its findings reveal shortcomings in my account, some of them those of oversight or neglect of available evidence. For example, while it is perfectly true as charged that Democrats openly used illegal tactics against the Populists, the dissidents did not keep entirely clean hands themselves. While I did say that "Populists retaliated in kind to some extent," that does not adequately acknowledge the extent of third-party violence and terror later uncovered by Barton Shaw, for example. In politics as in war, retaliation in kind is the rule rather than the exception, and I should have been more alert to expect it. For another thing, both parties sought black votes, and while the Populists made many more concessions to black interests and sensibilities, they showed much more zeal for protecting the rights of black Populists than of black Democrats and could be as rough in intimidating those who voted the wrong way as were their opponents. In short, there was not as much difference in political morality between the two parties as I sometimes suggested. Nor were the oppressed and the oppressors quite as neatly divided along party lines. These faults must be candidly acknowledged. Still, while "there was indeed plenty of 'thought control and racist bigotry and lynch-spirit,'" as I have pointed out, "the Populists were far more often the victims than the perpetrators."

The strictures of one prominent school of critics aimed at the historical reputation of Populism will not be addressed here, for the reason that I have dealt with them earlier in an essay called "The Populist Heritage and the Intellectual" and do not want to repeat myself. These critics were urban and Eastern liberals and intellectuals of the 1950s who were seeking an explanation for the McCarthyite assault upon the standards of decency and a scapegoat for their disenchantment with the seamy side of democracy. Many of them fixed upon Populism and its provincial supporters as the source of all that was retrograde and reprehensible in the democratic heritage. Among the burdens heaped upon the back of the old Pops and their alleged progeny were anti-Semitism, Anglophobia, Negrophobia, xenophobia, crypto fascism, jingoism, isolationism, imperialism, paranoid conspiracy-hunting, anti-intellectualism, and the assault upon privacy—these among others. Here, I felt that it was the critics rather than the defenders of Populism who bore the responsibility for historical error, and that the biases of provincialism had undergone a shift of geographical center to wind up on the Hudson River. But I have stated my reasons for these conclusions, as I have said, elsewhere.

Among the small circle of New York intellectuals I came to know I must have seemed something of an oddity—a professed champion of the Populists, one who even hailed from their haunts and retained more than a trace of his native accent. Very few of the New Yorkers had ever ventured south of the Potomac, or if so their South was Miami, much as their West was the Coast. The unexplored hinterland was the habitat of bigots, anti-intellectuals, and reactionaries—McCarthyites. My reception among the New Yorkers, mainly during teaching visits at Columbia, owed much to a long friendship with Richard Hofstadter. We met in Washington the year after the war when he was teaching at the University of Maryland and I was doing research at the Library of Congress. He joined the faculty of Columbia the next year and I that of Johns Hopkins, but we kept close ties. It was an improbable bond, this tie between the Arkansas-bred, Georgia-Carolina educated provincial and the cosmopolitan city-bred intellectual. The friendship, however, was never threatened by our differences, either of origin or of views. They were assumed rather than debated. But on the beaches at Wellfleet, in winter breaks in the Caribbean, a summer together at Oxford, and during frequent exchange of family visits there occurred over the years a meeting of minds that transcended provincialities on both sides. We continued to differ, but not enough to prevent agreement on an extensive editorial collaboration, a multi-volume Oxford History of the United States that was left for me to continue alone after his tragic early death.

But to return to the biography, my treatment of the last years and the horrors of the Mr. Hyde phase of Watson's life enjoyed comparative immunity from negative criticism. Perhaps this relative immunity may be due to more than absence of error. Part of it, I suspect, was attributable to the confirmation that the Mr. Hyde picture gave to prevailing expectations. Here at last was just what one might expect as the sorry denouement in the life of the typical Southern demagogue, and it also fed certain preconceptions of Populism mentioned above. This, of course, is speculation and may be unfair to the critics as well as possible merits of the biography.

One corollary of the Populist critique of the 1950s deserves attention at the risk of some repetition. That is the alleged tendency, stressed by Richard Hofstadter, for Populists to degenerate on aging into cranks, nuts, and zanies, or what he called "deconversion from reform to reaction." Tom Watson would, of course, be a classic example, were this the rule. I felt constrained, however, to question any partisan correlation between zaniness and Populism. If I must bow to a critic who complains that I have "tended to make readers forget that there was more to a movement than one leader," I must enter the same complaint with regard to zaniness and reactionism.

Thinking back over this youthful first venture into print and the treatment it has had during five decades, I realize that despite the warm critical reception it originally enjoyed (which I have neglected here), how much a book for the times and of the times it was. It was a book *for* the 1930s and *of* the 1930s, a book for hard times and hard scrabble, when rebellion was rife and the going was rough. It was a time when mutinous voices were heard in the land, voices that seemed echoes from the 1890s, often the same rhetoric reflecting much the same conditions and outrages. It was a book for the Okies and the Arkies, who were the rednecks and the lintheads and the Sambos further down the road now but no nearer salvation. It was also a book of, as well as for, the provincial at odds with the metropolis, for the colonies against the colonizers, for the exploited against the exploiters, and perhaps, at unguarded moments, one for a partly imagined past against a very real and hostile present. It was certainly not the book I would have written later, probably not even the same subject I would have chosen later. If that confession winds up on the brink of skeptical relativism, it by no means dismisses the worth of the enterprise or the lessons in history learned—at least the lessons the author learned from writing history and biography.

Chapter 3

By Sea and by Land

T HE YOUTHFUL historian's choice of a second subject
is a critical decision, for it usually projects a future course
and may even shape a career. Assuming he does anything more at all, will it be more of the same, an elaboration of
the first, or will it be a departure into new directions? As it
turned out in the instance at hand, the choice did not prove to
be the historian's to make. The subject forced upon me could
hardly have been more different from the first or more unexpected. But I did not know that at the time I thought I was
making the choice, nor for some time thereafter.

The search for a subject for the next book began early in 1938,
even before the first was published. Biography had proved so
fascinating that it seemed only natural to try another one. In
April, 1938, I found myself writing Howard Beale to ask "who,
if anyone, is writing a biography of Eugene Debs . . . a possibility for my next job. Of course he greatly interests me, as
you know, and I would ask nothing better than a chance to do
him." Beale encouraged the idea as did others. But counsel on

the choice of subject was divided. Maury Maverick, who had written to suggest collaboration with him on a book about Southern leaders, wrote in October of the same year, "Lay off of Debs. You must be a red, or a Communist—or maybe an anarchist or something. Leave Debs alone—that is only an inhibition of yours. What we must do is rescue the South. . . . Go to it at once—get started on the idea of writing the ten leaders. It is exactly the right idea." I nevertheless continued to pursue the Debs project and went to Terre Haute, Indiana, in December to interview surviving members of the family and to inquire about the Debs papers. The inquiries in Terre Haute put an end to the project, since it was made perfectly clear by Debs's brother that the papers were not going to be made available—to me at least—for some years to come. I felt that I could not wait that long.

Before other alternatives could be explored, within a couple of months in fact, came a letter from Charles Ramsdell, then editor of the projected *History of the South* series, inviting me to do the volume on the New South. This flattering offer was somewhat giddily accepted on the assumption that it provided entry for me as a mole to subvert the establishment. It was a questionable decision on the part of the editors to risk such an assignment in the hands of a youth just turned thirty. Rarely does a historian, accustomed as he is to reading correspondence about the fateful decisions regarding the future of others, have the opportunity of reading such letters about himself. It happened, however, that a student of mine much later explored the editorial correspondence concerned and shared his finding with its subject, much to my edification. The editors did, in fact, appear to have taken their responsibilities seriously and found predictable doubts to overcome. This prospective author was so young and so impressionable, and rather erratic to boot. But in the end they decided to take the risk, in spite of the obvious fact that "Woodward can't write."

I already knew that Benjamin B. Kendrick had accepted the assignment and was presumably the editors' first choice. I then learned that he had withdrawn and recommended me. Writing to thank him and to say how pleased I was, I added, "But now that I actually face it, it looms up with staggering difficulties and problems. Where, for example, is the monograph output of a generation of seminars on the period? . . . I know you will agree that this volume will require more spade work than any of the other nine." Nevertheless, I professed to be "eager to get at the job."

Had I known then that twelve years would pass and that four intervening books would be written before the New South book appeared, I would doubtless have been less sanguine and might have bowed out for the same reason I abandoned the Debs project—that I could not wait that long. Apart from the extensive research required, I will not attempt to account for the dozen years of delay except to say that they involved three changes of academic address and four jobs from East to West Coast and back, three summers of teaching at Florida, Harvard, and Chicago, plus three years of duty as an officer in the United States Naval Reserve in the Second World War. In spite of all that, I was not entirely diverted from the long task. In June, 1941, I was writing a friend from Study Room 174 at the Library of Congress Annex that "I have had the most enjoyable and profitable four and a half months since February that I can remember," that I felt "more assured and excited about the job." With two and a half months to go I wildly predicted I could "finish up essential research work and possibly get a little writing done this summer. . . . I hate getting all tumescent with creativity about the end of summer and then being packed off to California for teaching."

It would be another whole decade before that book appeared, for within six months came Pearl Harbor and more diversions and delays than I had counted on during the next four years. After getting a naval commission and training at Quonset Point that led to qualification as a combat naval air intelligence officer, I was discovered to have written a book and ordered to report to the Office of Naval Intelligence in Washington. There my duties for most of the next three years consisted largely of writing more books. This was not in connection with Samuel Eliot Morison's official history of the naval war, but in an outfit assigned the duty of getting out to the fleet brief classified accounts of battles in small books or booklets as quickly as feasible after the actions occurred. *Combat Narratives* the series was called. So it was that my second book was not the result of my choice at all, but of military orders—as were my third and fourth books. For as it turned out, I wrote three such books, two of them classified "Confidential," printed without attribution of authorship, with circulation strictly limited to qualified personnel within the navy. Only one, the last written, was released for publication and brought out by the Macmillan Company, which had published my first book. This one was called *The Battle for Leyte Gulf* (1947). That was the official name covering four battles fought between dawn of one day and dusk of the next in three bodies of water covering five hundred miles, all waged in repulse of one huge final operation by the Japanese Navy. It was the greatest naval battle of the war and the largest and most complicated ever fought on the high seas.

Quite by coincidence, therefore, it happened that I was to write more naval history—a subject quite remote from my center of interest—than any other single kind of history. The experience, however, could not be dismissed as lost time. I came to regard it, in fact, as an important part of my education as a historian. The strenuous exercise of mind in a completely strange and highly technical field of history induced a new respect for precise and reliable information, exact timing, and the infinite complexity of events with large consequences. This was history as pure action written almost entirely as narrative. Yet for all their technological complications, modern battles on the high seas are still human events. The historian soon found himself dealing with such familiar categories as personality, accident, luck, ambition, stupidity, and human error, even national character—factors that often proved more important than weaponry, fire power, and numbers. It is rare that a historian gets to know so many of his protagonists. The two colossal failures at Leyte Gulf are reasonably attributable to an American Hotspur and a Japanese Hamlet. It was a gratifying part of the naval experience to learn that the historian, with his old-fashioned compass, could find his way in deep blue water—surface, subsurface, or air—as well as on dry land.

Valuable as it proved to be for me as a historian, the naval history experience was more a diversion than a fulfillment. Its products, though winning praise by professional navy critics, were of no real lasting consequence, led to no further work in the field, and deserve no further attention here. I have related the episode mainly to account for delay in fulfillment of other intentions and to record another stage in my education as a historian. The center of my historical interest and purpose, however, remained throughout the war the long-delayed book on the South, now seven years past the starting point.

The prospect of a return to teaching in California, so far removed from archival sources, meant further delay. My great immediate need after the war ended was an academic base in the East, the closer to Washington the better. It was wonderful good fortune that just at this juncture Johns Hopkins University came forth with an offer. My good fortune was not limited to this proximity to the Library of Congress, but included the university's rather special policy of generosity and status for young scholars in their most productive years who wanted to pursue active scholarship. That meant, among other things, a research seminar in one's own special field and light teaching duties. At last the path ahead seemed clear. Once again, however, I failed to anticipate another unscheduled book, the fourth it became necessary to write before getting around to the one originally intended to be the second. But the necessity for the next intervening book was not to become apparent until much later.

In the meantime progress on the larger work went forward in an atmosphere highly congenial to scholarship. The re-

search seminar attracted able students who were soon pro-
ducing papers and eventually publishing books that contributed not only to their professional advancement but to the
progress of their mentor's project and to his own education as
a historian as well. There were times when it was hard to keep
up with them. The training of graduate students in my own
field became my main academic duty thereafter. And the intellectual family of former students expanded over the years to
form a bond of friendship and mutual criticism.

The plundering of Washington's libraries and resources was
supplemented during leaves of absence and summers by for-
ays into all the important archives and collections of the
Southern states from Virginia to Texas, with two summer terms
teaching at Cambridge and Chicago permitting the rifling of
New England and Midwest libraries.

Note files expanded inordinately with materials on all parts
and periods of the era to be covered, but as time passed and I
mined more and more archives, the file on or around the year
1877 grew disproportionately thick—bulky beyond any reasonable need for the purpose at hand. The editors of the series
had fixed the dates to be covered by the volume, 1877 to 1913,
and had not consulted this author's wishes. I might well have
chosen different points to begin and end, but I was hemmed
in by contract and by preceding and succeeding volumes. But
then every history book has to begin and end somewhere, often arbitrarily, and the assigned dates for this one had some
feasibility. The beginning date at least made sense in that it
marked the end of Reconstruction and the start of a new era
with the Compromise of 1877.

The traditional account of the so-called "Bargain of 1877" was
a familiar one, telling of desperate last-minute meetings, the
Wormley House Conference, between Republican friends of
Rutherford B. Hayes and representatives of the Southern states
to assure the peaceful inauguration of Hayes. His claim to
election by a majority of one electoral vote was bitterly disputed. According to the story, Hayes's friends had agreed to

abandon the two remaining Republican state governments in the South and give up future use of force to protect freedmen in exchange for Southern Democratic cooperation in the peaceful seating of Hayes and promises of protection for freedmen's rights in the South. Thus conceived, the Compromise of 1877 took its place in the standard histories as the last of the four great compromises of the nineteenth century by which peace between North and South was maintained or, in this instance, restored and reunion cemented. Early on, I began to suspect that things must be rather more complicated than this story suggested, especially if, as it appeared, the Republicans at Wormley House were giving up something they no longer possessed in exchange for something they had already secured and the Southerners were accepting something previously secured by other means in exchange for commitments already made. What kind of a bargain was this, anyway? I promised myself a closer look later on.

It was not, however, until I unpacked and tried to sort out that bulky file of notes on 1877 and earlier that the full complications of the subject began to dawn upon me. Clichés like "a can of worms" or "rabbit in a briar patch" were inadequate. This was more like a sack full of jigsaw puzzle pieces, parts of several puzzles, with many pieces missing, all jumbled together, yet somehow related. How to get them together? How to make a picture with them? What were all these letters from San Diego, Philadelphia, Sacramento, and Texas doing here? Why all the correspondence from chambers of commerce, boards of trade, cotton exchanges on the Gulf of Mexico, East Coast, West Coast, Middle West, from New Orleans, Chicago, Memphis, St. Louis, Vicksburg, Kansas City, Cincinnati, Atlanta? How did cabinet members and Supreme Court justices get involved with the mightiest railroad tycoons of the time such as Huntington, Gould, and Scott? Why did elaborate compromises between Union Pacific and Southern Pacific and between Central Pacific and Union Pacific happen to coincide with *The* Compromise between North and South? How did all this rhetoric about "The Road to India" and "a railroad to Mexico" fit in? Why were the main officials of the Western Associated Press so deeply involved in the negotiations? It was all very well to remember that this was the Gilded Age in its heyday, but how did civic hopes and private cupidity mesh with the national crises?

One peculiarity of the Compromise of 1877 soon became clear: unlike those of 1820, 1833, and 1850, which were openly debated and widely published, this one was privately negotiated and never officially published. Several of the participants later published memoirs with titles promising revelations that were not forthcoming: one a "Secret History," another an "Inner History," and a third an "Inside History." But they dealt with surface aspects or were couched in ostentatious reticence. An early scholarly monograph existed, but it was about the disputed election of 1876 rather than the Compromise of 1877. There were reasons for reticence. The correspondence of insiders was sprinkled with such sentences as, "This need not in fact could not be an open thing," or "I want to say things I cannot write," or matters that could not "be trusted outside of a narrow circle," or by Hayes's closest friend on things he did "not feel at liberty to write, even here."

It is unlikely that the puzzle would ever have yielded to direct attack, for so many of the missing pieces turned up by chance in improbable places over the years while my work on the big book went forward. The relevance of one piece of evidence, or one event, or one person to another often became apparent accidentally, and the accidents were sometimes years apart. I began to think of evidence as clues, people as suspects, and my role as that of detective. The problem was tantalizingly irresistible, but the solution continued to be elusive. It was not until the summer of 1949 that research in the Middle West, particularly in Des Moines, Iowa, and further work in Fremont, Ohio, began to bring things together. The elusive solution seemed at last to be within grasp.

The whole story would simply have to be told. But how? I could only spare one chapter for the subject in the book, and that would not be enough space. My first thought was a long article for a learned journal. That I started, but it got too long. The next idea was to write two articles or more, and I tried to sketch them out. But the pieces plainly belonged together as one continuous narrative. After much resistance I gave up and admitted that this had to be a whole book. By this time I was more than ten years beyond having started what was intended to be the "second" book. That one would have to be postponed again, since it was obvious that the book on the Compromise needed to come first so that it could be summarized and referred to in the other. The long deferred other was virtually finished, except for this part, but it had to be shelved once more.

Reluctant as I was to undertake the intervening book, which was to bear the title *Reunion and Reaction*, the writing of it proved to be more fascinating than any other I have written. The main reason, I think, was the shift from the customary role of historian as recorder-reporter to the more active role of historian as detective. There is some of that in us all, and in much of our work, as my colleague Robin Winks has shown in his book *The Historian as Detective*. But here all those latent impulses were called forth by a subject crowded with intrigue, concealment, connivance, dissembling, plot and counterplot, hidden motives, bribery, betrayal, and cover-up. In sum it added up to a mystery to be solved. With real detectives—that is, fictional ones (the only ones we know)—the denouement is a confession or conviction, usually concluding with a triumphant flourishing of the incriminating evidence. With the historian in a detective role, there are thrills along the way with discovery of clues, of course; but the denouement is slower in coming and does not arrive until the pieces are put together in the book. So the main excitement of the adventure comes in the writing. The historian-detective does not really know how it all turns out until he reads what he has written. If, indeed, he ever really knows, for there are elements of uncertainty in this, as in all other kinds of history.

Whatever the shortcomings and flaws in *Reunion and Reaction*—and I will get around to them next—the critical reaction of the historians reviewing the book on its publication in 1951 was quite favorable. Their response was obviously influenced by the appeal the story had for the detective in them. To Henry Steele Commager, it was "the story that is fascinating, a story as complex as one of Miss Dorothy Sayer's early mystery stories." For David M. Potter, it "solved not only one of the most baffling but also one of the most important mysteries of the American past." And Rupert B. Vance thought it "reads like a detective story."

Quite apart from the mystery-story appeal, the book had other assets inherent in the subject that served it well. For one thing the interpretation and much of the massive evidence were quite new, which always helps. Then too, the subject unavoidably addressed the moral core of national history, the abandonment of Reconstruction and with it many of the hard-won fruits of the Civil War in the Fourteenth and Fifteenth amendments, and the abandonment of the freedman's fate to his former masters. With powerful extraneous interests involved from coast to coast, with a presidency and the peace of the Union apparently at stake, with prominent roles assigned some of the most colorful, flamboyant, and unscrupulous figures of the nineteenth century, it could hardly fail to make a good story. With these assets to bank on, the book seemed to lead a charmed life for twenty years or more and began to be referred to embarrassingly as the "orthodox" interpretation. That dubious accolade is usually a sign of trouble to come. And come it did.

Serious critics did not get around to the deeper sources of the book for more than two decades. One reason for the delay was that retracing the tracks of the original research in the extensive and widely scattered manuscript sources took a bit of doing. First among the more serious efforts was an article in the *Journal of American History* by Allan Peskin pointedly entitled "Was There a Compromise of 1877?" Since the article was entirely addressed to *Reunion and Reaction*, the editor of the journal broke with precedent and invited me to reply in the same issue. The reply is available there under the title "Yes, There Was a Compromise of 1877," and it therefore seems unnecessary to give more than the barest outline here. Peskin's main argument in support of his contention that there was no Compromise was that several of its parts were never fulfilled. I point out that, on the other hand, even more parts of the Compromise of 1850 were forfeited or forgotten, whereas the most important parts in 1877 were fully realized. Indeed, that the latter compromise lasted longer than all the others put together. While my critic maintained that the Republicans "honeyfugled" the Southern Democrats, I contended that it was quite the other way around, and that the Southerners did the honeyfugling.

Within the same year that Peskin's article appeared, 1973, though completely uninfluenced by it, Keith Ian Polakoff published his book, *The Politics of Inertia: The Election of 1876 and the End of Reconstruction.* He "emphasized at the outset," he wrote, that his purpose was "not to refute Professor Woodward's work," that, after all, "the negotiations he described did take place," and that our differences over their importance arise in part out of difference in historical perspective. While Woodward was "concerned with the economic policies of the South's political leaders," Polakoff was "interested in the configuration of power in nineteenth century political parties." A well-informed and judicious study, it persuaded me that in the larger perspective he was closer to the truth about the determining forces than I. It was good criticism. I was struck especially by a quotation he used from a letter of Henry Adams to Samuel J. Tilden. "My own conclusion," wrote Adams, "is that history is simply social development along the lines of weakest resistance, and that in most cases the line of weakest resistance is found as unconsciously by society as by water."

The third and most effective critique of the monograph was a long article in the *Journal of Southern History* by Michael Les Benedict entitled "Southern Democrats in the Crisis of 1876–1877: A Reconsideration of *Reunion and Reaction.*" It was buttressed by two charts, two statistical tables of Guttman scale analysis, two appendices with analyses of forty-three roll calls, and three times as many footnotes, massive ones, as pages of text. It shunned no sources, neglected no data, unearthed fresh evidence, and applied appropriate methods of quantitative analysis. An all-out major effort, Benedict's critique scored valid points, required significant revision, and deserved respectful attention. It is the sort of criticism a historian dreams of—only to wake up in a cold sweat. To summarize Benedict's criticisms briefly, he maintains that I "described accurately a Republican effort to break down Democratic unity in the South," but (1) that this effort was "not the determining factor" in bringing about Hayes's inauguration, (2) that I overestimated the part Southerners played in moderating Democratic opposition, (3) that I also exaggerated the railroad lobby's part in influencing Southern votes, and (4) that I overplayed the threat of organized violence among Democrats to resist the seating of Hayes in the White House.

My response to these four points, without elaborating, is that I think Benedict is generally right, though we might differ on the degree or the significance of my exaggerations. He tempers the wind slightly by incidental compliments on "beautifully crafted chapters," but in so doing risks suggesting literary felicity as a source of embarrassment. Another critic, Terry L. Seip, who shares some of Benedict's strictures, also speaks of "a tribute to the craft of the author" but at the same time complains of the skill with which he "sprinkles his account with qualifiers and disclaimers." I can understand the annoyance. Qualifiers and disclaimers were, indeed, liberally and deliberately sprinkled about, admittedly with hope of guarding against vulnerability to this line of attack. I was, for example, careful *not* to say what "the determining factor" was in seating Hayes and careful to acknowledge that Home Rule was always the main concern of Southern Democrats, whatever the hopes of railroad lobbyists. Nevertheless, these anticipatory precautions do not let me off the hook. If what I wrote could give intelligent critics the impressions they received, they were right in calling me to terms. It is perfectly possible, of course, to suggest or imply interpretations and conclusions without actually stating or endorsing them, merely by the proportion of attention or space or dramatic content assigned to the evidence. To charges of this character I enter a plea of *nolo contendere*.

There are other legitimate criticisms that, so far as I know, have been neglected or underplayed. If I may enter the game myself, I think there are a few worth mentioning by way of anticipating further critics. One has to do with the origins and nature of the study, particularly the fact that it was the by-product of research for another book, the one on the New South, and not undertaken for itself. In the larger enterprise my interest was in discovering the character, identification, motives, and alliances of the leaders of the new order in the South. The crisis over the Compromise did much to illuminate that subject, but the focus upon it led to some distortion of emphasis and to some neglect of other participants, for example Northern Democrats, who (as Polakoff politely pointed out) did not receive the close study given the Southerners. A second criticism also concerns disproportionate emphasis and attention, this on the role played by Tom Scott's Texas and Pacific Railroad, its rivals, allies, and supporters. This was an entirely new story, one of much intrinsic interest, and one that constituted a fascinating part—though not the only part—of the detective game. None of these qualities (and certainly not mere novelty, however exciting) justifies disproportionate attention, but together they help explain that flaw.

Another flaw arose out of the author's current reaction against the so-called consensus school of historiography. That aversion partly explains the tribute deliberately paid to the late Charles A. Beard in the "Acknowledgments" prefacing the book, which was also a defiant announcement of adherence to some then-quite-unfashionable tenets of economic interpretation and a lingering attachment to a much denigrated historian who had gone out of fashion. One of my own students, Robert Sharkey, had already upset part of the Beardian interpretation of Reconstruction. But I permitted my loyalty to take me to the point of elaborating a Thermidor passage on the Compromise quite reminiscent of Beard. It now strikes me as derivative and overextended, as do some, though not all, of the allusions to economic motive in the interpretation of history.

Thinking back over this latest diversion of purpose by an unanticipated book, I do not find it in me to lament or disavow the effort. I would not write such a book in the same way now, or perhaps even twenty years ago, but that can also be said of earlier and later works. To concede that economic interpretations have sometimes been overstressed, however, is not to concede that economic motive is unimportant, much less absent. The latter assumption can also lead to distortions in history. Granted that *Reunion and Reaction* assigned material interests too large a role and too much space, that does not mean that they were not powerfully present or that they should have been ignored. Moreover, and by no means least, the close-up, inside picture of them at work in 1877 might incidentally have provided revealing insights on America in the Gilded Age— as well as on the sort of forces shaping the New South.

And finally, one reflection on the dual purpose in writing history—the portraying and the explaining. Both are important and they inevitably go together. They should not be confused, but they are difficult to keep apart, and one should not be allowed to crowd out the other. *How* events happen can be as important as *why*. Even if Henry Adams was right that the determining "line of weakest resistance is found as unconsciously by society as by water," the intrigues and plots and hopes—even those not fully realized, those hidden or not avowed—that people resort to in their confused efforts to shape the course of history can be as revealing about the meaning of the event as disclosure of "the determining factor." If, indeed, that is really ever fully or conclusively disclosed.

Chapter 4

Origin of *Origins*

"HOW CAN YOU possibly write so long a book," asked a friend, only half humorously, "about a period in which nothing happened?" He was referring to the book I had undertaken to write on the period of Southern history between Reconstruction and the First World War. We were sitting on the steps of the Library of Congress and the conversation went on till closing time. His question, however serious, reflected a prevailing popular impression about the post-Reconstruction era that was stuck with the name New South. Historians had so far done relatively little to correct the idea that nothing happened and that there was really not much to say about what did happen. Compared with shelves upon shelves of books that lined the Library of Congress stacks in the sections on the Cotton Kingdom of slavery, the rise and fall of the Confederacy, and the Reconstruction period, the existing bibliography of the period following was, apart from a few monographs, discouragingly short, thin, primitive, and immature.

My reply to my friend's question about nothing happening was that the shortness of the shelf was no measure of the period's significance and no indication that little had happened worthy of note. Taking the offensive and turning the tables, I contended that, in fact, the three previous periods mentioned had received an altogether disproportionate amount of time and attention from historians. After all, the antebellum Cotton Kingdom, the Confederate nation, and Radical Reconstruction were a succession of lost causes, ephemeral experiments of relatively brief duration. The Confederacy lasted only four years, and the Radicals less than an average of three and a half in the states involved. Taken all together from the beginning of the Cotton Kingdom to the end of Reconstruction, the three lost causes spanned only about three quarters of a century. That was the number of years already covered by the era whose foundations were laid in the 1870s by the so-called Redeemers, and as things turned out, still had a few years to go. Granted that all causes are lost in the end, did the longest and most durable one not deserve somewhat more attention than it had received?

In addition to the prejudice of low esteem for the period and the deficiency of scholarship on which to build, there were other problems. The title for the book, because it was to be one of a series, had been assigned or inherited—*Origins of the New South*, followed in monograph fashion by the dates, 1877–1913. I was glad to see the definite article before the word *Origins* dropped, and I very reluctantly accepted the *New South* and the coercive dates in the prescribed title. But I was also stuck with the term *Origins*. The word recalled a brief essay entitled "The Idol of Origins" by a martyred hero of the time, Marc Bloch of the French Resistance, foremost French historian of his generation. One trouble with *origins*, wrote Bloch, was the unavoidable ambiguity of the term—whether it meant *beginnings* or *causes* or was a "cross-contamination of the two meanings." Bloch continued, "In popular usage, an origin is a beginning which explains. Worse still, a beginning which is a complete explanation. There lies the ambiguity, and there the danger!" In his time, said Bloch, he had seen *origins* grow from a *preoccupation* to an *obsession* and in many cases a *demon*, which was "perhaps, only the incarnation of that other satanic enemy of true history: the mania for making judgments."

What an incubus of fallibility and temptation I had fallen heir to! How could I cope with it? One solace at least was the knowledge that Marc Bloch himself had used the forbidden term in the title of his greatest book, *Les caractères originaux de l'histoire rurale française*. His essay on "The Idol of Origins" was, in fact, a sort of apology. He began it with a memorable sentence: "It will never be amiss to begin with an acknowledgement of our faults." With the humility of the master in mind, I reflected that neither could it be amiss to begin forewarned of fallacies to be avoided. It was perfectly obvious that Bloch's "satanic enemy of true history" was still at work upon my own generation and that I enjoyed no immunity from "the mania for making judgments." I was even dimly aware of a personal propensity for it. Moreover, the very subject I was addressing seemed in a peculiar way to cry out for the making of judgments and thereby to compound the temptation. How much could I, or should I, resist the "satanic enemy"?

I have pointed out earlier some ways in which the legitimacy of the New South regime—and in my view the legitimacy of the social order still in place in the 1950s—was dependent upon a special reading of history. I would go so far as to say that the cornerstone of the New South—to borrow a figure from Alexander Stephens about the Old South—rested upon historical assumptions that constituted a veritable credo of the region. To question those assumptions at any point was not only to make judgments about history, but to pass judgment on the legitimacy of the social order sustained by the assumptions questioned. Yet that seemed precisely what my researches and my convictions disposed me to do.

Among the significant tenets of the New South's historical credo, first in importance was an image of Reconstruction as

61

betrayal, humiliation, and horror; as the work of radicals, carpetbaggers, scalawags; and as Negro rule that resulted in corruption, misrule, and degradation. Following this came the flattering image of Redemption, the overthrow of the Radical regimes, and restoration of Home Rule. The evils and excesses of Reconstruction not only justified the violence and fraud by which Redemption was achieved, but also the repudiation of all principles of Reconstruction, or as many as possible. Since Redemption was seen as salvation, the Redeemers were viewed as heroes. And since they proclaimed their work a restoration, the new leaders were assumed to represent a return to power of antebellum leaders of the old type. In contrast to the corrupt regimes of the Reconstruction period, the governments of the Redeemers were held to be beyond reproach, impeccable in their purity. Gratefully, the once-divided whites rallied around their old Confederate captains, put aside all differences, and became a Solid South—one in politics, one in credo, and one in all matters of race. Rising above logic, they professed to be equally loyal to the Old South of the Lost Cause and to the New South of Yankee ideals and business and nationalism. The contentment and acquiescence of the Negro and the corrupt abuse of his votes justified his disfranchisement and segregation. The South's enthusiasm for the war with Spain proved that reconciliation and reunion had been achieved. The South was at last in step with the U.S.A. in patriotism, progressivism, and prosperity. In the meantime, obliging Northern capitalists were seeing to the industrialization and modernization of the regional economy to the benefit of all, but especially Southerners.

According to the orthodox historical credo, these marvelous and beneficent developments had come about without any significant break with the past. Properly understood, they were to be thought of as the fulfillment and continuation of ideals, convictions, folkways, and institutions deeply rooted in tradition. These roots were tested by Civil War and Reconstruction but held firm in the passing storms. Henry W. Grady put the dogma succinctly in the 1880s when he said the New South was "simply the Old South under new conditions." The same view was sustained in various ways later by professional historians such as Ulrich B. Phillips and Broadus Mitchell. Wilbur J. Cash in 1941 gave the doctrine its most popular and influential expression in *The Mind of the South*. The Civil War, he declared, left the old mentality "entirely unshaken" and instead "operated enormously to fortify and confirm that mind and will." This meant that "the Old South was preserved virtually intact," and "the pride of the old ruling class was not weakened but even distinctly enhanced." The new political leaders and industrialists came from "the old ruling class, the progeny of the plantation," and the common folk "never departed in the least from their ancient allegiance."

Within the historical guild of professionals, the orthodox views of continuity held predominant sway through the 1940s and received their most eloquent and extreme expression at the end of that decade in the presidential address of Robert S. Cotterill before the Southern Historical Association. "In no phase of the economic life," declared Cotterill, "was the New South new. . . . It was merely a continuation of the Old South. And not only in its economic life: the New South inherited, also, the *spirit* of the Old. It inherited the racial pride, and if anyone wants to call it racial prejudice, there can be no objection. . . . There is, in very fact, no Old South and no New. There is only The South. Fundamentally, as it was in the beginning it is now, and, if God please, it shall be evermore."

Merely to state in bare outline the tenets put forth in *Origins of the New South*, published in 1951, would be to repeat the orthodox credo backward or turn it upside down—a sort of historiographical black mass in the eyes of true believers. The blasphemy included the replacement of continuity with discontinuity, unity with disunity, and harmony with conflict. I do not mean to say that all historians of the period were true believers or rigidly orthodox, nor that I was the only one suspected of heresy. Nor would it be accurate to suggest that I was so simplistic as to believe there was no continuity, unity, or harmony at all and no truth in any of the dominant views then held. At issue, as in most historical problems of importance, were questions of emphasis and degree—not the existence of the phenomena under discussion. Although I did not set out with the deliberate intent of challenging all predominant views, I should have to acknowledge that the end product might reasonably suggest to some minds such an unworthy suspicion.

To start with the founding fathers of the new order, the Redeemers, who overthrew and replaced the Reconstruction regimes, they were denied the identity implied by the term *restoration*. Of course nearly all of the new rulers were old enough by 1877 to have established some roots in the old order, but it was my contention that, "In the main they were of middle-class, industrial, capitalistic outlook, with little but nominal connection with the old planter regime." In political antecedents, the combination of old parties under the Conservative name brought the Whigs into prominence, and in policies the Redeemers leaned to business, wealth, and commercial sympathies. The Redeemers thus represented more innovation than restoration, more break than continuity with the past.

Instead of the orthodox record of scrupulous honesty attributed to Redeemer governments and contrasted so sharply with the corrupt record of Reconstruction, I found these new administrations disgraced by numerous state treasury embezzlements and defalcations, sordid deals, public land scandals, and blatant favoritism. More continuity, at least with Reconstruction, was ironically manifest along these lines than along others. Most disgraceful was the common practice of leasing state prisons and convicts to favored politicians for exploitation as a private labor force. Instead of the white loyalty and political solidarity supposedly inspired by Redeemers, third-party rebellions and bitter division over economic and political issues faced the new administrations from the start. After a brief suspension of revolt in the 1880s, more powerful and wide-spread rebellions erupted under Populist party organization in the 1890s.

Instead of industrialization and cotton-mill construction under the benevolent paternalism of old planter types as pictured in New South historiography, the new Southern captains of the cotton-mill industry were found to be predominantly hard-nosed entrepreneurs bent on large profits and distressingly indifferent to the well-being of their white labor force, largely women and children. Much the same genus presided over the new fortunes in mining, lumber, heavy industry, tobacco, and railroads. The New South creed, intoned in the chorus led by Henry Grady, proclaimed a gospel of reconciliation between estranged races, classes, and sections, a miraculous melding of Old and New South ideals. But it proved in fact to constitute a capitulation, a celebration of the values, standards, aims, and interests of the new masters. *Reconciliation* was only a code word. As the editor of the *Industrial South* put it in 1885, the New South message was a belated acknowledgment and a cordial admission that the South, like the rest of the country, was destined "to be peculiarly a community of business men."

In this vein the revisionary subversion was repeated throughout *Origins*. The reconciliation of the farmer meant subordination to the status of tenant or sharecropper and the degradation of poverty. The reconciliation of the black freedmen meant their submission to the demands of white supremacy, including disfranchisement, segregation, and loss of civil rights. The reconciliation of labor meant the lowest wages and most degraded standards in the country. The reconciliation of the sections meant local control for the Southern elite and the South's political subordination in many federal matters to the Northeast. Investment, development, and modernization by Northern capital, more fruits of reconciliation, meant a colonial status for the Southern economy. For the region as a whole per-capita wealth in the first decade of the new century was about half the national average, and per-capita income about 40 percent lower than the national average. Distribution of the better things of life—health, education, and the standard of living—in the colonial economy reflected not only these gross disparities between the South and other regions but also appalling inequities within the region itself.

This summary has not paused for elaboration or minimal concessions to opposing views, nor has it suggested the numerous cautionary reservations and exceptions and hedgings inserted to guard against charges of extremism. Without them it sounds more dogmatic and polemical than it was. If it revives the familiar charge of relapse into quaint and outdated Beardian patterns, I should point out a significant departure I made from that path. Beard had framed his classic economic and political conflicts in interregional terms—North versus South, industrial versus agrarian, free labor versus slave labor, and so forth. My picture included in the frame large components of intraregional conflicts—strife within the South itself, discord between forces that were equally Southern on both sides. This alteration, of course, served to sharpen rather than blunt my assault upon orthodox views.

The reception of *Origins* when it finally appeared late in 1951 brought surprises and puzzlement. Was I rightly understood? Or had I subdued and qualified my tone too much? Instead of voicing expected indignation and protest, predominant responses ranged from tolerance and respect to unqualified applause. This was even true of the later reviews in learned journals. Perhaps I had misjudged my professional colleagues. There were exceptions, to be sure, such as the regrets of one reputable member of the guild that I had not "shown a greater measure of sympathy for Southern traditions and for the essential goodness of long-suffering people." Or another who felt I had gone "to the other extreme" and emphasized "economic and racial conflict to the exclusion of everything else." But these were relatively rare exceptions to the rule.

A source of continued puzzlement and some concern was

the silence of negative critics and the failure of serious criticism to appear for years following. The absence of criticism, if it lasts long enough, can be as disturbing as being ignored—though admittedly in a different way. It can mark the superannuation of a book. The critical silence continued ominously for some two decades. In a preface to a new edition published in 1971, twenty years after the first and entirely unrevised, save for an updated bibliography by Charles B. Dew, I remarked that revision "must be the task of others," very likely a historian with "another world view, fresher insights, and perhaps a dif ferent philosophy of history." I added that "it would already appear to be time for him to be about his work." Instead, I was confronted the next year with a full-length reappraisal of the book in the *Journal of Southern History* by Sheldon Hackney, a former student then in his more impressionable years. It was his conclusion in 1972 that "the pyramid still stands," that there had been "no major challenge," that the book had "survived relatively untarnished through twenty years," and that most monographs in the field since 1951 "reinforce much more than they revise about *Origins of the New South*." He went so far as to suggest the highly tentative explanatory hypothesis that, "One possible answer is that Woodward is right about his period."

I wish it were possible for me to go along with such an attractive hypothesis, even to embellish it with the theory that the evidence was so massive, the logic so conclusive, and the writing so persuasive that the conclusions were irresistible. Quite apart from the questionable tenability of such theories, however—as Hackney himself pointed out, "revisionists have never been noticeably deterred by the absence of serious flaws in the body of knowledge they wished to revise"—there is an alternative if less-flattering explanation that I find more persuasive. The period of Southern history from 1877 to the 1950s, despite changes within it, was the longest era of reasonable stability in the nineteenth and twentieth centuries. Toward the end of that long period, in the 1930s and 1940s, it is not surprising to find historians and laymen alike taking much stock in the predominance of continuity and unity in Southern history. The assumption was that basically things had always been pretty much that way. It was only in such a period that Cash could have come forth in 1941 with his remarkable summation of the prevailing consensus, or that Robert Cotterill could have set his words to the meter of the doxology in 1949.

Given such firm commitments to the old doctrine of continuity, what happened to delay for so long criticism of a book that took the very opposite line? What happened, I think, was less the persuasiveness of the book than a change in the times, a series of drastic changes. In the 1940s the South suddenly entered a period of nearly three decades filled with more shocks of discontinuity than any period of its history, with the possible exception of the 1860s. Part of them are caught in the familiar litany—cotton moving west, cattle moving east, blacks moving north, Yankees moving south, everybody moving to town, and towns and industries growing faster than ever before. Old monuments of continuity disappeared in rapid succession: one-party politics, one-crop agriculture, one-horse farmers, the white primary, the poll tax, Jim Crow signs, disfranchisement laws. Out they went. In their place came the *Brown* decision of 1954 against segregated schools, the Civil Rights movement and black nationalism, the collapse of massive resistance, and at the demand of a Southerner in the White House a new and comprehensive Civil Rights Act and a Voting Rights Act. With all that pandemonium of contemporaneous upheaval and daily change of the "unchangeable" during the fifties, sixties, and into the seventies, what was there left to say about continuity? I know the present is not supposed to affect our reading of the past, but in this instance I think it did. In fact I think it had much to do with the charmed immunity from criticism that *Origins* enjoyed for so long.

At any rate the old chorus of continuity fell silent, and 1951 turned out by chance to be a fortunate time to gain a hearing for a different tune. The old orthodoxy of continuity yielded much ground to revisionists who emphasized the importance of change in Southern history. It was even possible in 1955 to begin a book on the Jim Crow system by writing that "the people of the South should be the last Americans to expect indefinite continuity of their institutions and social arrangements," that while others had "less reason to be prepared for sudden change and lost causes," the South's historical experience was different and distinctive.

It was an intellectually exciting experience to be restoring the neglected third dimension of change to the relatively flattened two-dimensional picture of Southern history. The oncoming younger generations joined eagerly in the enterprise, and their new monographs poured from the presses. It was great while it lasted, but I knew that it could not continue in health and vigor without the stimulus and challenge of genuine criticism. That was not to come on in full cry until the 1970s—certainly soon enough to forestall premature superannuation of *Origins*.

In the meantime it was gratifying to witness the beginnings of criticism around my own seminar table as early as the 1950s. To mention a few examples, there was Robert Sharkey, *Money, Class, and Party* (1959), who upset the Beardian concept of Republican economic motives that I inherited. Earlier criticism did not derive from ideological but from methodological, mainly quantitative, techniques that had been unavailable to me. Applying these techniques as well as conventional sources, Sheldon Hackney's *Populism to Progressivism in Alabama* (1969) offered a more realistic view of both movements; and J. Morgan Kousser, *The Shaping of Southern Politics* (1974), corrected errors of mine as well as some of V. O. Key's. Quantifying critics were at work at other seminar tables as well. One example of the more effective was Carl V. Harris, who demonstrated in the *Journal of Southern History* that my metaphor of "Right Fork, Left Fork" to characterize the South's sectional politics was much too simplistic so far as congressional voting was concerned.

The main thrust of criticism in the 1970s and 1980s, however, was ideologically oriented, whether quantified or not.

This orientation was not tied to right or left. Instead it embraced representatives of points across the whole political spectrum who reflected in some degree a common return to the old pre-1950 orthodox ideology of continuity. Some were more orthodox than others, but in spite of sharp differences between them I shall lump them all together as the New Continuitarians. The return to continuity is perhaps not so clearly related to a change in the times as was its temporary abandonment. But as soon as the hurricane of social, political, and economic change had subsided in the 1970s, as soon as the Civil Rights Movement and the Second Reconstruction were ended and repudiation begun, a new orthodoxy in race relations was established, and something like social stability was restored— the chorus of continuity took up where it had left off a generation before. The discontinuity of Continuitarianism had only been temporary—*continuity interruptus*. The New Continuitarians often sounded much like the old, cited the same works and used many of the same arguments. So numerous are their contributions to the critical literature on the thesis of discontinuity that it is impractical to treat them all and only possible to sample them.

Since continuity nurtures tradition, minimizes change, and fosters respect for the past, it has a natural appeal for conservatives. It is significant that a new organization of conservative historians in 1980 should have given their journal the title *Continuity*. Conservatives of the guild are generally less ready than radicals to proclaim their leanings. With no desire to apply unwanted tags to individuals, I shall confine my comments to specific works and *their* leanings. One early critique from this side is William J. Cooper, Jr., *The Conservative Regime* (1968), a low-keyed and civil reminder that the Redeemers of South Carolina, at least, as represented by Wade Hampton, would have liked nothing better than to have restored the old order with some concessions. Which was true enough, if a bit impractical. Cooper does concede that "the Conservative regime welcomed industry and capitalists," and he even acknowledges that cooperation was pretty close between Conservatives and industry, and that their chief editorial voice, F. W. Dawson, equaled Grady as a New South tub-thumper.

A bolder and more direct attack was an essay called "Redeemers Reconsidered: Change and Continuity in the Democratic South, 1870–1900," by James Tice Moore in 1978. Weighing "the contending forces of continuity and discontinuity, tradition and innovation," he comes down firmly on the side of continuity and tradition, dismissing departures from the old order as superficial. He contends that the Redeemers represented no change of guard and that the old "traditionalist, agriculturally oriented elites grasped the New South as firmly as they had the Old." Granting that they recruited a few "outsiders, parvenus, and adventurers," so did "the England of Charles II or the France of Louis XVIII, yet there can be no denying that restorations of a sort took place in those countries. The same is true of the Redeemer South." While Moore concedes that the indictment of Redeemer economic policies and pro-business bias in *Origins* is "convincing in its main thrust," he feels that the book is much too hard on the Redeemers and deplores its interpretation as "iconoclastic, even cynical in tone." The stress on the infamies of the convict-lease system, public-land and railroad swindles, tax exemptions for business, favors to speculators, and monopolies to the Louisiana State Lottery overlooks the rewards of economic development, public benefits, and large state revenues derived from these sources. Also overlooked were the blessings of huge cuts in tax rates, more than 80 percent in one state, and "massive tax savings" for property owners generally. Benefits for the propertyless and the freedmen are not explored, nor are losses to state treasuries from defaulting and absconding Redeemer treasurers.

One entirely new dimension of continuity, incidental to the subject, comes from the conservative journal *Continuity* in the spring of 1981, an essay by Grady McWhiney entitled "Continuity in Celtic Warfare." Since the "Celts constituted an overwhelming majority in the South," they managed to carry on down to the Civil War folkways first noted by the Romans at a battle in 225 B.C. The Rebel yell lifted at Shiloh and Gettysburg, it seems, was first heard by the Roman legions more than two millennia ago.

Critics on the left, with no apparent awareness of a common cause with allies on the right (and with other fish to fry), also enlisted under the banner of continuity. The two examples noted are of the Marxist persuasion, and both are fellow-travelers of the continuity line, though they arrive at quite different destinations. They differed from each other as well as from travelers on their right. The quotation marks in the title of Dwight B. Billings, Jr.'s *Planters and the Making of the "New South"* (1979) anticipate his conclusion that it was "hardly new at all." How could it be if, as he finds, the old planters took charge after the war and largely planned, owned, and managed the industrial South on into the twentieth century? The sample on which his finding is based is North Carolina, with emphasis on the cotton textile industry. Since the old aristocracy took the lead in industrializing the economy, North Carolina, like some European countries, took the "Prussian Road" of modernization by aristocratic elites. Billings finds support in the old-school Continuitarians Broadus Mitchell and Wilbur Cash. He quotes Mitchell and his brother approvingly as saying that in the South "the pioneers of industry were generally gentlemen. Not operatives or mechanics as in England, they did not see themselves as seizing mean advantage," but were instead "moved by the spirit of noblesse oblige" much as were "manorial lords of the early middle ages." While the governing law of industry "outside the South was the impersonal market," writes Billings, Southern industry "by contrast, stressed communal values. Its image for social relationships in mill villages was not the market but the paternalistic family." He takes special pleasure in quoting Cash on the identity of Old and New South and the continuity of the one with the other. Historians who emphasize change and discontinuity are snared in "the romantic tradition," while Cash, he declares, was "right on target."

Also from the left comes Jonathan Wiener, *Social Origins of the New South: Alabama, 1860–1885* (1978), and he too finds that the old planters not only survived but prospered and dominated the New South as they had the Old South. Still in the saddle, booted and spurred and armed with hegemony, the Alabama planter elite, however, charged off in the opposite direction from that supposedly taken by North Carolina planters. Instead of taking the lead in modernization and industrial development, they took a socially reactionary line and proved an obstacle to growth in manufactures, industry, and commerce. Wiener's most interesting and scholarly contributions to the ongoing discussion are the statistical data he dug out at great pains about the "persistence" of landholding among the large planters in five counties of the western half of the Alabama black belt from 1850 to 1870. Of the 236 planters with the greatest wealth in landholdings in 1860, 43 percent "remained in the elite in 1870," as compared with a "persistence rate" of 47 percent in the previous decade. Moreover, the wealthiest among the wealthy persisted in larger percentage. This is all based on retention of acreage of land. Granting devastating losses among all landowners in the South, he finds that "the planter elite in 1870 was relatively wealthier than it had been in 1860." That may have been cold comfort to the "relatively" blessed in view of the 67 percent decline in the average value of land per acre in Alabama, and the total loss of capital invested in slaves, or the 60 percent loss of all capital invested in agriculture, not to mention all investments in Confederate bonds and paper, and the huge debts concealed by land titles. But it is on this basis that Wiener contends that "war and Reconstruction did not significantly alter the antebellum pattern of elite persistence and social mobility."

Although much remains to be cleared up—how typical is the Alabama sample, for example, and how reliable was 1870 as a stopping point (with 1873 coming up) for measuring persistence—I nevertheless think Jonathan Wiener was justified in challenging Roger Shugg's phrase, "revolution in land titles," and my quoting it to describe "the downfall of the old planter class." I still believe something that can be called a revolution occurred and that in the process the planter class took a terrific tumble. The question becomes how significant are land titles, many of them heavily debt-encumbered, in measuring the persistence of wealth and power. If one is interested in "relationships to the means of production," as Marxists regularly are, I think other questions will arise. For example, how many of the old planters who hung onto or inherited land and prospered are known to have moved to town, opened stores, run gins, compresses, and banks, invested in railroads and mills, and played the speculative markets. My suggestion is that those members of the old planter families who made it to the top in the new order very likely took that course. And in becoming businessmen they transformed themselves into members of the new class that was creating a commercial revolution and fostering an industrial revolution. They might still call themselves planters, as might any townsman who foreclosed on land for debt. Most towns boasted a "Merchants and Planters Bank." But land at depressed values, crops at depressed prices, and labor with 30 percent lower productivity were not the real sources of power, nor were celebrated genealogies.

Wiener is not entirely blind to these realities. He notes that the percentage of large landholders listing their identifying occupations as other than "planter" multiplied five-fold in one sample, and he speaks, for example, of John B. Gordon and Alfred H. Colquitt as being "secret industrialists." They certainly made no secret of it, though, for Gordon's numerous ventures in railroads, manufactures, mining, and real estate were advertised, not concealed. Together with Colquitt, Gordon and his brothers cleared $1,000,000 in speculations in less than a year. To describe General Gordon as "the living incarnation of the aristocracy of the Old South" misconceives his antebellum origins as well as his postbellum career. On all these

74

matters the neo-Continuitarians of the left would profit from thoughtful reconsideration.

Between the left and the right are those of the center who have shifted back toward the old orthodoxy of continuity or become fellow travelers of the neo-Continuitarian line. Like the radicals and conservatives, the liberals also return for support to the old classics of the tradition, but for the most part they have been content to correct what they take to be recent overemphasis on change and discontinuity. For example, George B. Tindall, *The Persistent Tradition in New South Politics* (1975), announces as his "central theme" the idea that "a thread of continuity ran through the transition from Bourbonism to Progressivism in the New South," with Populism linking the two. But it is only "a thread" and not a hempen rope that he chooses for his metaphor, and his thread is knotted into a Hegelian triad of thesis, antithesis, and synthesis. The last is supplied by the Progressives, who "built into their synthesis" of Bourbonism and Populism "the persistent tradition of community in the South." Even then, he modestly declares that this is only the theme of his book, not "that it is the central theme of southern political history, nor that it will resolve the complexities of the subject."

A more explicit example of a return to the old orthodoxy of continuity from the centrist position is found in Carl N. Degler, *Place Over Time: The Continuity of Southern Distinctiveness* (1977). As the title of his book indicates, he is addressing two themes, that of distinctiveness as well as that of continuity. But he makes it clear at the start that the latter is his main concern and that distinctiveness is incidental to it. "I want to emphasize," he writes, "that my purpose in discussing distinctiveness is to demonstrate the essential continuity of southern history." More specifically, he writes, "My intention in this book is to demonstrate the continuity in southern history that has been either explicitly or implicitly denied by recent historians of the South like Woodward, Genovese, and Gaston."

Degler's premise is that continuity is "closely related to the question of distinctiveness" and that he can "show the continuity of southern history" by proving that the South became distinctive quite early and has remained so all along. If his premise is correct his case is proved. Few historians of the South, and certainly not those just named, would deny the region's distinctiveness. Without it there would be little point in writing of the South separately from the rest of the nation. The question is the logic linking distinctiveness with continuity. The fact is that the former can and has been maintained without the latter and that difference can and has been enhanced by change—by discontinuity.

After elaborating upon the standard constants of climate, soil, and geography, about which there can be little argument, Degler settles upon slavery as "the basis of southern difference." Since it was slavery "that made the plantation possible," the two institutions "laid the foundation for the South's distinctiveness" and assured the continuity of Southern history. Did the abolition of slavery, then, not mark a break of discontinuity? He seems to be of divided mind on this question. First he says that "the ending of slavery did not mark a major break in the continuity of southern history," but a few pages later he writes, "One must admit that the abolition of slavery marked a significant change in the lives of southerners, white as well as black. Certainly it was a discontinuity in southern history." He manifests the same indecisiveness about the Civil War and its consequences. In a previous book, *The Other South*, published in 1974, he writes that "out of that war came not only devastation, but also the destruction of slavery and the society that rested on it." It might be assumed that the destruction of a society and its foundations could be the occasion of some historical discontinuity. Three years later, however, in *Place Over Time*, after saying, "The Civil War was certainly a discontinuity in the United States," he can write in the same paragraph, "It is my contention that the end of the Old South did not mark a significant break in the flow of southern history; it was only a minor disruption, with limited effects." Apparently it was the Old North instead of the Old South that bore the brunt of discontinuity. While admitting "the undoubted contribution of Reconstruction to southern distinctiveness," he contends that this "should not cause us to overlook the continuity between the antebellum years and those after Appomattox."

Like fellow travelers of the continuity line on his right and on his left, Degler derives support for his thesis from older Southern prophets ranging from Grady to Cash. Citing Henry W. Grady, Daniel Augustus Tompkins, and Richard H. Edmonds, he quotes the latter as saying in 1903, "The South of today, the South of industrial and railroad activity, is not a new South, but a revival of the old South." It was perhaps inevitable that Degler should also cite Ulrich B. Phillips and that he should conclude triumphantly with a quotation from Wilbur J. Cash.

On the other hand, the incoming tide of continuity historiography already shows signs of turning. The criticism of the thesis of discontinuity and change has not all been negative and some of it lends strong support. For example, Harold D. Woodman in a forthcoming paper speaks of "massive changes following the Civil War" as "a revolutionary transformation" of the South's economy. "I use the term 'revolutionary' advisedly," he writes. "I mean a fundamental, radical transformation in Southern history." He has little patience with the advocates of "planter persistence" and planter dominance in the development and industrialization of the New South.

While Gavin Wright regrets that the controversy has been defined as continuity versus change (as do I), he leaves no doubt about his own views. In *The Political Economy of the Cotton South* (1978), he emphasizes not only the massiveness but the suddenness of change as well. "The South," he writes, "was wrenched out of one historical epoch and into another during the decade of the Civil War." The transition "involved a basic change in the character of human relations" and "the loss of financial independence" on the part of farmers. Changes

77

of this extent have happened "elsewhere in history," to be sure, "but they represent the kind of long-run development" that is associated "with basic legal, institutional changes evolving over decades and centuries. In the South, it happened overnight, historically speaking." His conclusions have been greeted as emphasizing "the basic coherence and continuity of Southern economic history," but they do not sound that way to me.

Similar conclusions about the revolutionary character of post–Civil War change in agriculture are reached by Michael Wayne, *The Reshaping of Plantation Society* (1984), a study of the rich Natchez district where there occurred "a profound break between the plantation regime of the old order and the plantation regime of the new." Barbara Fields, *Slavery and Freedom on the Middle Ground* (1985), discloses revolutionary alterations in the lives of Maryland freemen and freedmen, as well as the old master class. Numerous other studies point toward similar conclusions. One that addresses the question of the old planters' role in industrialization deserves attention. David Carlton, in *Mill and Town in South Carolina* (1984) and elsewhere, challenges the thesis of "continuing planter hegemony" in the New South industry as "a serious misinterpretation of postbellum Southern history." In South Carolina, the prime exhibit of Old South continuity, he shows by detailed statistics that planters and farmers "played distinctly minor roles in mill development" and could be said to dominate in only two of a hundred firms. New men, mainly small-town businessmen with vital Yankee help, ran the industrial show.

No end to the debate seems yet in sight, though it threatens the exhaustion of patience. Monographs, articles, published debates and rebuttals, conferences, symposia and their collected papers continue to proliferate. No comprehensive treatment of them is possible here. *Origins of the New South* is cited frequently as the take-off point of controversy or the source of misguided theses. Nowhere in the 1951 volume, so far as I recall, however, are the terms *continuity* and *discontinuity* counterposed to announce or frame a thesis. Admittedly the issue arises repeatedly, with emphasis usually falling on change, but the emphasis derives from substance rather than theory. In the preface to the 1971 edition, in speaking of changes that had overwhelmed the South during the two decades since 1951, I did remark that the South had been "long unique among the regions of the nation for abrupt and drastic breaks in the continuity of its history." Perhaps the provocation derives as much from that as from the substance of the book. Of course, I do not shoulder or claim all the blame, for other historians, including economic and econometric historians have pitched in freely. They are free to share what consolation may be had (besides that of being "right") from the belief that stirring up controversy can be an incidental service to scholarship.

But could not this debate have been shortened by some such reflection as those found in Carl Degler's concession that "all questions of continuity are relative," and that "all history is a combination of varying degrees of continuity and change"? It probably will be in the end, as banal as that solution is. But that does not dismiss the significance or deny the value of the controversy. For most of the important debates over history, as I have remarked earlier, have not been about absolute but about relative matters, not about the existence but about the degree or extent of the phenomenon in question. Evidently there have existed deep differences of opinion over questions of that sort in Southern history that needed airing.

Chapter 5

Race and Rebellion

MUCH HAS BEEN MADE of time and place and ideas as influences on the writing of history. A neglected influence is the reader, usually regarded not as an influence but only as an object to be influenced. Every historian, however, must begin with some conception of the readers he is addressing. The consequence is a considerable measure of reader participation in the writing. Does the writer conceive of his readership as small or large, specialized or general, knowledgeable and sophisticated or naive and uninformed, sympathetic and receptive or antagonistic and skeptical? The answers the writer postulates to these questions will necessarily influence what is written and how it is written—style and tone, as well as substance. Not only the reader, the writer, and the subject, but the complex of interrelations among all three are involved in shaping the writing of history.

I am specially aware of these relationships in thinking back over the writing as well as the curious reception of *The Strange Career of Jim Crow*. The most curious thing is that although it was written for the smallest of audiences it gained the greatest number of readers, an enormous number compared with any other book of mine, more perhaps than the total number of readers of all the other books put together. In short, I had badly misconceived my readership. There were awkward and unforeseen consequences that deserve attention.

The book originated as a series of lectures I gave at the invitation of the University of Virginia in October, 1954. The dedication of the first edition reads, "To Charlottesville and the hill that looks down upon her, Monticello." The audiences consisted of a hundred or so people, academic though unspecialized, and overwhelmingly Southern. I was not a stranger there, for I had served on the university faculty briefly some years earlier. There was no distinction between the audience and the readership conceived for the book, since the manuscript for the lectures became copy for the printer. Publication had not been assured at the time of the lectures, and I made no mental distinction between audience and potential readers.

The readership conceived under these circumstances definitely contributed to the nature of the book. I knew perfectly well that there was much I did not have to explain to such an audience in speaking about the history of race relations in the South. They shared a common background and a lifelong familiarity with a thoroughly, universally, and legally segregated society, a system that had then prevailed little changed for many years. It seemed unnecessary, therefore, to spell out fully either the enormities and excesses of the system or many of the subtleties and nuances of racial relations under that system and in its background. Such knowledge was assumed as part of a heritage common to both speaker and audience.

A summary of the book would be impractical here, and I shall have to be content with quoting one sentence in which I much later attempted to set forth its thesis: "Briefly stated, the thesis was, first that racial segregation in the South in the rigid and universal form it had taken by 1954 did not appear with the end of slavery, but toward the end of the century and later; and

82

second, that before it appeared in this form there occurred an era of experiment and variety in race relations of the South in which segregation was not the invariable rule." The thesis was advanced guardedly, with elaborate qualifications and repeated insistence that it did not postulate any golden age of racial relations in the past.

I could assume that my audience would hear me out with the degree of tolerance then prevailing in Southern academic circles—and perhaps a bit more for being under that shadow of Monticello. But I did not assume any ready acceptance of my thesis about segregation. Instead I assumed an audience resisting this doctrine and clinging rather to the prevailing, almost universal Southern belief that the system of segregation (however regrettable) was firmly entrenched in remote origins and quite beyond the possibility of change by legal action. To understand the implications and the contemporary shock of a challenge to that faith, it is necessary to explore the milieu of the mid-1950s in which it was conceived and delivered.

I wrote the lectures in the summer months immediately following the Supreme Court's unanimous decision in the case of *Brown* v. *Board of Education of Topeka* on May 17, 1954, declaring racial segregation in the public schools unconstitutional. Awaited with tense apprehension and dread, the *Brown* decision nevertheless did not immediately touch off explosive resistance. A year of grace was promised before the Court would act on implementation of the decision. In the meantime optimists pointed to the South's relatively peaceful compliance in several states—at least on a token basis—with earlier Court decisions on the admission of blacks to juries, school boards, voting booths, white-collar jobs, and as students in some colleges and universities. Whites had also begun to move over grudgingly to make room for a few blacks in professional athletics, military barracks, dining cars, and Pullman cars. Might this not also happen peacefully in public schools, especially if, as expected, federal judges in Southern district courts postponed compliance?

Sober reflection would have discounted such optimism. The *Brown* decision on public schools struck a more sensitive nerve than earlier ones had ever touched. Furthermore the decision was more sweeping in its implications, for it appeared to remove the constitutional underpinnings of the whole segregation system and strike at the foundations of Jim Crow law. It was the most momentous and far-reaching decision of the century in civil rights. At least part of the South's initial mildness of response could be attributed to incredulity: the spontaneous belief that such things simply could not be, the conviction that the Supreme Court was demanding the impossible. That conviction rested firmly on the universally cherished interpretation of history holding that present racial relations, including legal segregation, were of ancient origins, going back to slavery and beyond, entrenched in the folkways of both races, a product of the natural order of things, and therefore impervious to change by legal enactment, as proved by unfortunate experiments during Reconstruction.

Any challenge to that orthodox Southern interpretation of history, particularly in such critical moments as those of 1954–1955, when regional solidarity was so important, could be deeply disturbing. Especially so if such heresy originated in the South itself. Yet here in one of the most respected Southern universities, at its invitation, a historian of supposedly reputable standing who claimed to be of Southern birth, rearing, and education dared ring all the changes of unorthodoxy and then publish them in book form. What sort of Southerner was this, anyway, and how did he go so thoroughly wrong? What had got into him? There were disturbing rumors of his deviant connections in New Deal days. Which brings us to the next historiographical question: the author's background and commitments. I will attempt to deal with these questions with as much objectivity and detachment as is possible under the circumstances.

It must be acknowledged that my personal origins would seem to make me a most improbable candidate for the role I later chose to play. Born and reared in rural and small-town Arkansas of a family with a slaveholding background, I came along during the era when white racial orthodoxy and oppression were at their very peak and the revived Ku Klux Klan was most active. I have heard students of race relations in South Africa, including South African scholars, say that the system in the American South was much harsher then than it was there. My parents were academics of modest status, my father a public school administrator in Arkansas and later head of a small college in Georgia. They were not happy about the racial injustice of the times, but they were not outspoken about the matter. Little in those Arkansas years would seem to help explain the incipient rebellion of the future historian.

In 1928 I transferred to Emory University from Henderson, a small Arkansas college, for my last two undergraduate years. There in the shadow of Stone Mountain, where the Klan had been reborn thirteen years before, the pattern of white racial orthodoxy was not very different from that of my native Arkansas. In Atlanta, however, through my uncle, Professor Comer M. Woodward, I saw a good deal of Dr. Will Alexander, head of the Commission on Interracial Cooperation, and his associate Arthur Raper. They encouraged my interest in racial problems, though they were themselves cautious and conservative in their approach to them.

Quite as significant were the associations I made, while I was teaching in 1930/31 and 1932/33 at Georgia Tech, with faculty members across town at the all-black and segregated Atlanta University. Of particular importance was my acquaintance with a poet and writer, J. Saunders Redding, a young instructor of my own age and the first black man with whom I ever broke bread and exchanged views as an equal. That did mark a turning point. It was underscored by my acquaintance with the young black poet Langston Hughes in New York during a year of study at Columbia in 1931/32. Through Hughes and his friends, doors were opened to me for an inside look at the Harlem Renaissance and a brief membership in an amateur Harlem theatrical group with whom I took a role in performance of a play. An approach to W. E. B. Du Bois with a proposal to write a thesis on his ideas had less fortunate results. His *Souls of Black Folk* had deeply moved me. An interview in his editorial office at the *Crisis* got nowhere, however, after he heard that Deep South accent of mine.

The following summer I spent in Europe, mainly in France, Russia, and Germany. In all three countries the young traveler was struck by the display of protest against the plight of the Scottsboro blacks falsely accused of rape charges in the courts of Alabama. A month in Germany, living with a Jewish family in Berlin, during the same summer of 1932, the eve of Hitler's coming to power, brought home dramatically the ominous political abuses of other "racial" prejudices.

Back at Georgia Tech after the New York and European adventures, I encountered a new and bolder experience in race relations. This arose out of the case of Angelo Herndon, a young black Communist charged with violating a Reconstruction death-penalty statute against inciting to insurrection. Herndon's offense was leading a demonstration in Atlanta against a cut in relief to the unemployed. Here was another Scottsboro case developing in my own city. At a meeting of the A.F. of L. Labor Temple, I was elected vice-chairman of a committee for the defense of Herndon. The committee's main function was to raise funds, and to that end a mass meeting was called and very well attended. In the course of it, however, the chairman, a woman of high social position and head of the Atlanta Socialist local, suddenly resigned on account of Communist party intervention in the case and left me holding the bag. My services to the Herndon committee were soon terminated by my departure from Atlanta after losing my job at Georgia Tech. I had been officially admonished for my activities though not, I believe, actually fired because of them so much as because of a drastic budget cut that affected many other junior faculty members as well. At any rate, I departed the next year for Chapel Hill somewhat the wiser, but still with much to learn about race relations.

Not that segregation, of all the many terrible problems that black people and the South faced, was the most important or most urgent, but it did nevertheless come to be the dominant public racial issue of the time. This was largely because of the growing intervention of the courts and Southern white resistance to their decisions against the Jim Crow system. That system had reached its perfection in the 1930s and prevailed throughout the South in all aspects of life, everywhere one looked. Southerners of the present generation who grew up after it disappeared may well wonder how their elders could have daily made their way back and forth through this anthropological museum of Southern folkways and pronounced its wonders perfectly normal. Yet with rare exceptions, gentry and humble folk alike, not excepting men of learning, saw nothing extraordinary about the scene, or if so they kept their counsel. Everywhere one was assured that this was the way things had always been, that it was because of Southern folkways, that colored people themselves preferred it that way, and anyway there was nothing that could be done to change it.

To see it as it actually was often required borrowed vision, particularly a look through foreign eyes. There was the little English girl who, on seeing a drinking fountain clearly designated "Colored," eagerly turned it on, only to be disappointed by the flow of ordinary uncolored water. It is noteworthy that the first writer to succeed significantly in removing the scales from native whites' eyes was a foreigner, the Swedish scholar Gunnar Myrdal, author of *An American Dilemma* (1944).

A new and extraordinary foreign perspective came my way during the Second World War while I was on duty as a naval officer in India. With a letter of introduction in hand, I sought out Dr. Bhimrao Ramji Ambedkar, acclaimed leader of India's millions of untouchables and later a figure of first importance in Indian constitutional history. He received me cordially at his home in New Delhi and plied me with questions about the black "untouchables" of America and how their plight compared with that of his own people. He also took the time to open to me the panorama of an ancient world of Indian segregation by caste and to show me how it appeared to its victims. Another foreign perspective came of a visit to lecture at University College London, early in 1954 and during the academic year following, as a visiting professor at Oxford. There I absorbed from British colleagues the views of American racial policies entertained by intelligent and respected opinion abroad.

Stimulating as the foreign adventures were, however, they were of minor significance compared with long years of back-home experience and increasing involvement in civil rights actions. I had published several books on Southern history, none of them specifically on racial relations though all of them necessarily gave some attention to the subject. In them may be found seeds and anticipations of the thesis in my *Jim Crow* book. But the earlier works were of a different character, addressed mainly to the scholarly or specialized readers and consequently of rather limited circulation and influence.

More indicative than scholarly monographs of things to come was the part I played in the early 1950s in the efforts of the National Association for the Advancement of Colored People (NAACP) Legal Defense and Educational Fund to gain hearing from the Supreme Court for its case against public school segregation. Counsel for the appellants in the *Brown* case supported by the NAACP were preparing a brief in response to an order of the court setting the school segregation cases down for reargument. At their invitation I met with members of the counsel, including Thurgood Marshall and Jack Greenberg, to assist in preparatory research, which included not only law but history and sociology. Both John Hope Franklin and I prepared monographs described by a Foreword to a reprint of the brief submitted on November 16, 1953, as "the history of reconstruction in the South and on the purposes and results of segregation." Both the historians were cited and quoted in the brief. As it turned out, the Court was more impressed by sociological evidence than by historical arguments, so that it is doubtful that the historians had much impact on the Court's decision on May 17, 1954. The point for the subject at hand is that the author of the history of segregation was publicly and thoroughly committed in a positive way on the judicial aspect of his subject within less than a year of his delivery of the lectures at the University of Virginia.

The association with John Hope Franklin has more than incidental or casual significance in all these developments, including my education as a Southern historian. We had met in the mid-1940s and quickly discovered many bonds other than common scholarly interests to bring us together. We had grown up on opposite sides of the Arkansas-Oklahoma border and, of course, on opposite sides of the race barrier. On his side he had seen the law office of his father burned by a mob, and on mine I had witnessed Klan and mob action. Franklin had pulled out of his provincial origins earlier in his career than I had in mine by going to Harvard for his graduate work. We compared notes on coping with Northeastern provincialism, but our immediate and pressing concern lay in coping with prejudices nearer home. On the personal side this involved what now appear absurdly elaborate conspiracies to get Franklin admitted—physically—into functions, conventions, and programs of his own profession in the South. Apart from rules, customs, and prejudices of white professionals, that often came down to exclusion from restaurants, hotels, and toilets. I had seen him go lunchless at libraries and disappear for hours merely to relieve himself. A crisis and a break with precedent came at a convention of the Southern Historical Association when I was president in 1952. An annual dinner was cancelled at a Knoxville hotel that refused to seat black members, and the entire membership was bused miles across the country to an establishment that agreed to serve them—Franklin and a couple of others. In all this, as in weightier collaborations such as the NAACP brief for the Supreme Court, or in later years related scholarly problems and professional crises, John Hope invariably combined perfect intellectual and moral poise with inexhaustible good humor and a big laugh that banished any inclination to heroic posturing. I naturally appealed to him for help in preparing the lectures on segregation and owe him much for the criticism his reading of the manuscript produced.

I was in England in 1955, when the Virginia lectures were published. The first year's sales of *The Strange Career of Jim Crow* in hard cover were unexceptional and continued so for a couple of years. Then remarkable things began to happen in the market that could not be attributed to the genius of the publisher's sales department or to newly discovered merits of the book. What happened in sudden escalation of sales can only be understood in terms of events quite beyond control of author or publisher.

The hushed restraint of incredulity over the *Brown* decision in 1954/55 gave way early in 1956 to something near panic across the South. The first violence was a riot in February at the University of Alabama over integration. Senator Harry F. Byrd of Virginia called for "massive resistance." In March of 1956, a manifesto against integration was signed by 101 of 108 congressmen from eleven Southern states. Citizens' Councils, organized to block enforcement, spread from Mississippi across the region. Six state legislatures adopted dozens of prosegregation laws in the first three months of the year, and others followed suit later, some with a view to closing public schools rather than desegregating them, others resorting to the historic fighting slogan of "nullification."

The lights of tolerance and reason and respect for the law began going out all over the South as the fever of rebellion spread. Books were burned, libraries purged, news suppressed, magazines excluded, TV programs withheld, films banned. Mob violence accompanied the first desegregation of schools in the border states of Texas, Kentucky, Tennessee, and West Virginia in the fall of 1956, and some cities closed their public schools entirely. Lower South states made no gestures of compliance at all and boasted of their defiance. Governor Orval Faubus of Arkansas in September, 1957, carried defiance to the point of using state militia to halt token integration at Little Rock. He withdrew his troops on court order, but their place was taken by hysterical, spitting white mobs who forced removal of nine black children. Whereupon President Eisenhower ordered in federal troops to enforce the law. That marked the first breach of the Compromise of 1877 in eighty years and the end of an era of Southern history.

In the meanwhile other age-old understandings and assurances began to fail the white South—the myth of Negro contentment with the "Southern Way of Life," for example. The successful year-long black boycott of Jim Crow buses in Montgomery in 1955/56 brought forward a national leader of black protest in Martin Luther King, Jr. Early in 1960, with the sit-in demonstrations in Greensboro, North Carolina, the great Civil Rights movement got underway with youthful black leadership from the South, committed to nonviolent principles, and attracted vast numbers of followers in the North as well as the South.

The Jim Crow historian was soon watching these developments from a new perspective. In the fall of 1962, just before the bloody battle at Oxford, Mississippi, over the admission of James Meredith to Ole Miss, I joined the faculty of Yale University. There I found students in a state of excitement, full of curiosity about the Southern movement, and many of them eager to fly to the aid of besieged black civil rights workers in the South. They held mass meetings, departed in busloads on "freedom rides" to the Deep South, and organized "Mississippi summers." In this exalted mood they watched the Battle of Oxford, the Birmingham atrocities, the murder of Medgar Evers, the March on Washington, the Selma March, and the Mississippi Summer outrages.

To be embraced publicly and enthusiastically, even by those one may admire, can inspire mixed feelings in certain sedentary types. Martin Luther King, Jr., was quoted as calling *The Strange Career* "the historical Bible of the civil rights movement." And as a member of the great throng of Selma marchers who listened to Martin King's eloquent speech in front of the Alabama state capitol, I heard him read and endorse passages from the book as support for his crusade. I say my feelings were "mixed" only because I knew perfectly well what those Montgomery white people who silently lined the streets were thinking and saying about a certain Yale professor of Southern origins being quoted by Martin King in those circumstances.

The whole thing was regarded from the Yale point of view and in most of the North as a Southern drama or tragedy, with the Northern students participating—quite sincerely as a rule—in the role of missionaries. Historically minded among them recalled the role of Yankee schoolmarms in the First Reconstruction. With the passing of the Civil Rights Act of 1964 and the Voting Rights Act of 1965, it seemed as if the end were in sight. Once more, just a century after the first instance, Northern intervention had put down Southern rebellion and brought freedom to oppressed blacks. In a mood of self-congratulation, Northern crusaders were about ready to lay down their arms—when suddenly, without apparent warning, black rebellion exploded in their own backyards with more violence than they had seen in the South. For four summers, from 1965 through 1968, the black slums in city after city were set aflame by looting and embattled mobs that left smoking ruins. More than 150 major riots and hundreds of minor disturbances occurred in those years. The worst, in Detroit, required 15,000 federal troops to restore order, left 43 dead, more than 1,000 injured, and 2,700 businesses sacked, half of them demolished.

What had been a lively curiosity about a remote regional problem suddenly swelled into an urgent demand for knowl-

edge and explanation of what was obviously a national problem—at times an obsession. And what had originated as a
modest communication to a Southern academic audience had
swelled into a mass paperback publication for a national and
quite mixed audience of vast numbers. It was a wholly new and
unique experience for an academic historian—this particular
one, at least. Where I had never thought of a readership in more
than thousands, I was now confronted with readers in the
hundreds of thousands. They were certainly not the readers I
had in mind originally, those for whom the book was written.
Nor were they the sort to whom there was much I did not need
to explain, who shared my background, who understood un-
spoken assumptions, and who did not require the spelling out
of certain subtleties and nuances.

The overexpanded readership included the truly uninformed who needed all the help they could get. They could not
be expected to pick up elliptical references, respond to sym-
bolic names, or readily distinguish the figurative from the literal. Given the strangeness of the subject and its history, many
were prepared to believe almost anything and more than a few
were truly naive. They often sought for the cheering and
hopeful message, the simple answer, the easy solution. A national debate was raging in the midst of a violent crisis in which
cities were quite literally aflame. Participants in that debate had
little time to read and those who did only had time to read on
the run. They sought quotable passages, to confirm views, advance an argument, make a point. They often discovered what
they sought and used it as they wished.

I found myself quoted or cited in editorials, articles, congressional debates, even judicial opinions, for purposes with
which I often sympathized. But I was appalled by the reckless
disregard for context with which the quotations were frequently used. The carefully noted exception, the guarded
qualification, the unstated assumption, the cautionary warning was often overlooked or brushed aside. Letters poured in
from unknown people who revealed appalling misreadings.

The most common was that the Jim Crow system, along with other racial injustices, was superficially rooted and could be readily eradicated by right-thinking reformers.

Other professional historians, noting some of these same phenomena, began to express doubts and misgivings of their own. Was not this book, hastily produced on the heels of the *Brown* decision, a new instance of "presentism," of viewing the past through the distorting lens of the present? Had the author waited for enough perspective and distance? Was he not too personally committed to a point of view? Could this be a reversion to the instrumentalism of early progressive historians? Did it not share the old quest for a "usable past"? Could it not too be described as history with a purpose, the purpose of solving current problems? Did it show sufficient respect for the integrity of the past? These questions were not always unfriendly; some were put obliquely, even sympathetically. But they were nevertheless troubling thoughts, no less so because some of them had occurred all along to the author himself.

The voice I listened to most attentively about these quandaries and tensions was that of an old friend who had the greatest right and the surest authority to speak. This was David M. Potter, by whose side I had sat through the first and only course in American history I ever took in college, in whose home I had visited in Augusta, and whose place I eventually took at Yale when he left for Stanford. In all our long friendship down to his tragic death in 1971 I never had cause to doubt his word or entertain any but the highest regard for his opinion. In whatever estimate he ventured of my writings—and he understood them thoroughly—Dave Potter was generous to a fault. Yet between the lines, more rarely in the text, sometimes in an aside or over a drink he would gently and sympathetically voice his misgivings. If the historian sets out to interpret the past to the present, may he not, he would suggest, wind up with the endless task of correcting present misconceptions to the neglect of reconstructing the past as it really was? If, as I reminded him, Tolstoy in *War and Peace* once compared the

grotesqueness of the modern historian with "a deaf man an-
swering questions no one put to him," Potter would mildly remark that they might have been asking the wrong questions
and that the historian might well turn a deaf ear and frame his
own questions of the past with due regard for what was important to the past. And might not a strong commitment to a
desired end create a dangerous tension between an ideological
commitment and a devotion to realism for its own sake?

The admonitions of my friend expressed a respect for the integrity of the past which I fully shared. I even doubted that if
the present did ask the right questions of the past and the historian could provide answers faithful to the record, this would
necessarily result in a "usable past" in the sense of solving
present problems. And certainly I agreed that usefulness to reformers and embarrassment to their opponents—or for that
matter embarrassment of reformers and usefulness to opponents—should never be regarded as an admissible test of the
validity of any historical thesis.

Less troubling—mainly because I could respond to them
publicly and had invited them—were learned articles and
books, often inspired by the *Jim Crow* thesis, some of them
supporting, but some taking issue with the author on scholarly grounds. Since I have already traced the history of this
controversy up to 1971 in *American Counterpoint*, it is not necessary to recapitulate here. It should be noted, however, that
these exchanges of differing views and criticism were con-
ducted with civility and invariably in a spirit of getting at the
truth. For my part, I responded in three revised editions of the
book, the last in 1974, almost twenty years after the original
edition. In them I not only sought to bring my account of rap-
idly developing events up to date, but also to respond fairly
and fully to criticism and new findings on the subject. Some of
the new findings I incorporated readily; some of the criticism
required alteration of emphasis or acknowledgment of error.
While active research continued in the field (as it still does),
while monographs multiplied and many questions remained

unsettled, I continued to believe that the essentials of the original thesis remained valid.

One theme of criticism more persistent than others was that I had overemphasized the role of law in the history of segregation. In support of this theme, critics held that I had relied too heavily on legislation as evidence of change and of periodization. Such critics took an anthropological view of the role of law in history, contending that it typically served to register formal support for custom, practice, and attitudes already prevailing rather than to change them. Since one of the main and most controversial points of the book was the relative recency of the segregation system, and since I *did*, in fact, stress the role of law, this criticism was of crucial importance. The critics who took this line naturally lent support to the orthodox Southern view that racial relations, including segregation, were of ancient origins and impervious to change by law either in the past or in the present and future.

My reply to this criticism was that although segregation had numerous precedents in custom, practice, and attitudes, the new laws were of profound significance. They rigidified practice, eliminated exceptions, and applied to all on the basis of race alone—race as perceived by any whites. The new laws took no account of status, class, or behavior of blacks, but applied to all alike. "The Jim Crow laws," as I saw them, "put the authority of the state or city in the voice of the street-car conductor, the railway brakeman, the bus driver, the theater usher, and also in the voice of the hoodlum of the parks and playgrounds. They gave free rein and the majesty of the law to mass aggressions." They did, I believed, have a very great significance and marked an important turning point.

Later scholarship in the field—too late to be used in the 1974 revision of the Jim Crow book—has given some ironic and instructive turns to the disputed thesis. In his *Race Relations in the Urban South, 1865–1890* (1978), Howard Rabinowitz has pointed out that prior to the establishment of segregation, blacks were simply excluded entirely, or very largely, from many public services and institutions. Since segregated facilities—even if very unequal and inferior—were better than none at all, segregation ironically represented a measure of progress for blacks and was welcomed by some and sometimes promoted by their party. I completely overlooked these ironic precedents, so preoccupied was I with the issue of segregation. The oversight illustrates the dangers of allowing present-day issues to shape or define historical investigation. Another deserved correction came from one of my own students, J. Morgan Kousser, whose study, *The Shaping of Southern Politics* (1974), though in general agreement on interpretation of the period, pointed out a high correlation between leaders of disfranchisement and black-belt wealth, as well as more active opposition on the part of blacks and less interest in the white counties than I had allowed.

Rather than diminish as popular interest declined, the controversy over the origins of segregation among scholars has widened and taken more sophisticated turns in the 1980s. A new dimension has been added by extending the investigation to comparative history, most notably by John W. Cell, *The Highest State of White Supremacy: The Origins of Segregation in South Africa and the American South* (1982). My interest in that subject had been whetted not only by George M. Fredrickson's excellent book, *White Supremacy* (1981), but also by a visit I made to South Africa immediately before the terrible explosion of violence in Soweto in 1976. Taking off from *The Strange Career*, Cell's comparison of the South with South Africa, "finds it hard to choose" between its interpretation and the revisionists, but thinks that "the debaters have talked past one another," and that "the revisionists have failed or refused to meet Woodward on his own ground," the "watershed" of the 1890s, where "his critics have largely avoided him." While Cell finds much to agree with on both sides, he seems to gain most illumination on his comparison between the American South and South Africa from *The Strange Career*.

I should not take leave of the continuing debate without mentioning an important expansion of the subject by Joel Williamson, *The Crucible of Race: Black-White Relations in the American South Since Emancipation* (1984). Already indebted to him for earlier revisions and insights, the controversy has been redefined by his latest contribution. While Williamson says that his conclusions are "essentially and vitally different" from mine, he also acknowledges many congruencies and is characteristically generous in expressing gratitude and indebtedness. It is impossible not to agree with him that "this is how the pursuit of truth in history works when it works well."

Before popular obsession with the subject subsided an unexpected turn of events added a final twist of irony to the career of Jim Crow. No sooner had the demise of legal segregation been assured than a movement of black nationalism arose containing extremists who disdained or outright rejected integration into the white world. The development recalled the experience of earlier generations of historians who had focused their attention on slavery and emancipation, only to be reminded after the triumph of freedom that slavery was by no means the only problem or emancipation the complete solution for the problems of many black people.

I have been asked how, on looking back over three decades of controversy, criticism, and misunderstanding, I might feel about the whole Jim Crow venture in history-writing. Pressed for an answer, I would confess to feeling somewhat chastened and perhaps a bit wiser for the experience, but on the whole quite unrepentant. I readily admit the pitfalls and fallacies of presentists and instrumentalists, but decline to be classified among them save as an interloper. Rejecting identification as a fulltime presentist, I nevertheless hold that since the historian lives in the present he has obligations to the present as well as to the past he studies. The present always proceeds, consciously or unconsciously, on some theory about history, very often a false one; and it might turn for information about the past to sources less well qualified to speak than historians— even historians whose researches are incomplete, even on subjects that had not previously been investigated. After all, there has to be a first historian of any subject. Questions have to be asked before they can even be wrongly answered, and answers have to be ventured even before we are sure that they are addressed to the right questions. Errors have to be made before they can be corrected and contrary answers provoked. All of which leads to controversy, to be sure, but controversy is one of the ways we have of arriving at what we assign the dignity of truth.

Anyone who accepts such a challenge must be prepared to make mistakes, to take criticism, and to be corrected. My advice is to stay out of the kitchen if you can't take the heat. I will admit reflecting that one such venture per career is probably enough. I was sobered but not deterred by the dangers of undertaking research on a controversial subject about which I had strong convictions. I knew of historians who began study of very remote, even ancient periods of history with strong convictions, and I would guess that this is probably more the rule than the exception. History-writing is an enterprise fraught with dangers. As for the unanticipated encounter with a mixed and multitudinous and uncomprehending mass readership, I believe that worse fates have befallen academic historians—for example no readership at all. Large circulation is one of the hazards of the trade, but hardly the most perilous or prevalent.

With the full advantage of hindsight, therefore, I am on the whole undismayed by the experience and, while not without some apologies, I repeat, quite unrepentant. If foresight had been enriched by hindsight, I admit that I might have done it differently—and I am sure, more correctly. But I am more disturbed to admit that if hindsight had preceded foresight I might not have done it at all. And that would have been to miss an experience, an adventure, that I perversely continue to cherish.

Chapter 6

Shifting the Burdens

A T SOME POINT in a long career devoted to a specialized field of history, no matter how parochial its
bounds, the historian is tempted to feel that his findings have meaning and value for a larger public than his fellow
specialists and that he should share his arcane insights more
widely. It is a critical moment, a temptation best resisted until
wisdom ripens. It came upon me rather prematurely in the
1950s, however, and was to prove irresistible. What made the
temptation so irresistible was my fear of and revulsion for
the mood into which the country at large had fallen in that
decade and the policies, convictions, delusions, obsessions,
myths, and fallacies that mood had inspired.

A few words will recall some of the more prominent fea-
tures of the national mood in the 1950s. Americans of that time
had the feeling they were on top of the world and there to stay.
They had recently emerged victorious from great wars on opposite sides of the globe, wars in which they were sure their
cause was righteous and their hearts were pure. Once more

Americans had triumphed or vitally assisted in the triumph of the cause of justice, liberated the oppressed, and punished the wicked. Then they had generously rehabilitated stricken allies with a plan described as "not against any country or doctrine but against hunger, poverty, desperation, and chaos," and befriended former enemies.

Moreover, the liberators had come through the ordeal of fire with their homeland completely unscathed, their economy redeemed from a long depression and booming with prosperity. With Europe and Asia struggling to their feet, America dominated world markets. Forgetting their recent struggles with poverty and depression, Americans flaunted their famous standard of living. They took a model kitchen to Moscow as a soapbox from which to lecture Chairman Khrushchev. They advertised and drove their outsized automobiles in all streets of the world. America's technology was unsurpassed, American "know-how" legendary. Anything was possible. The impossible only took a little longer. America already lived in a postindustrial, postmodern, science-fiction future unattainable by less-fortunate folk and unthinkable to the Third World. Henry Luce called it "The American Century." Unified, confident, and powerful, Americans prided themselves on their military prowess, their economic productivity, their diplomatic triumphs, and the vindication of their high ideals. In this mood America presented herself to the world as a model for how democracy, power, opulence, and virtue could be combined under one flag.

These blessings seemed to entail certain obligations, among them that of serving as policeman to the world. Awkwardly and rather self-consciously, Uncle Sam assumed these duties. Uneasily conscious that the land of the free and the home of the brave was picking up the mantle recently dropped by Great Britain, our moralists lectured the mother country on the wickedness of imperialism. The new policeman on the beat was the friend of all liberation movements except those infiltrated by the new imperialists from Russia. Our interest in Asiatic and

African peoples lay only in their "development" and well-being. If it bore any resemblance whatever to imperialism, it might be called "welfare imperialism." In addition to guarding the welfare of these clients, the new policeman was keenly aware of the mischief created by the bully on the block, the USSR. He was known to have evil designs and pernicious ideas and must be kept under control. If the bully threatened to get out of hand, the new policeman did not speak softly and he carried a very big stick—the ultimate weapon, in which he enjoyed a temporary world monopoly. He had already proved that he could use it effectively.

Unparalleled power, unprecedented wealth, unbridled self-righteousness, and the illusion of national innocence—it all struck me as an ominous combination full of potential dangers to the republic. But it was only after an additional element in this combination was brought home to me that my concern became genuine alarm. This was the element of hysterical insecurity that resulted in the great witch-hunts of the 1950s—notably but not solely those of Senator Joseph McCarthy. It was brought home to me most closely by the invasion of my own university, then Johns Hopkins, and the victimization of my own colleagues and friends.

These alarm bells of the 1950s kept touching off in my mind muffled echoes from the Southern past of my special field of study. If I could somehow relate echo to alarm, I might find a way to bring to bear from my researches of the past some needed warning of the dangers that I perceived all around me. For the time being, however, I could see no way of bringing that about. My native South seemed to be as much obsessed by national delusions and myths as any other region, if not more so. And who could be persuaded to listen to fancied echoes from a remote provincial past at such a time as this, anyway? What I needed was detachment, distance, perspective, the establishment of some separate identity within the country yet immunity from its engulfing nationalism, a critical stance from which to attack the myths. With these preoccupations I entered upon two foreign experiences in the early 1950s, each of which provided unexpected illumination.

The first of these was teaching a seminar at the University of Tokyo in the summer term of 1953. I had accepted the invitation with the assumption that since the Japanese students could not be expected to know anything whatever about my field of interest, they could best profit from an elementary survey of Southern history. On proposing such a course, however, I met with an extremely polite but quite firm request that the subject matter be confined to the Reconstruction period. Puzzled by this manifestation of the mysterious East in the academy, I reluctantly agreed, still very skeptical about the wisdom of the decision. It was not until some weeks of the seminar had passed that I discovered what lay behind the insistence upon concentration on Reconstruction. For one thing the most popular movie in town was *Gone With the Wind*, and it had already enjoyed a long run. The Japanese, of course, were currently being reconstructed by the Yanks, and they identified with the defeated Confederates. They wanted to know what reconstruction was like from the South's experience. In these circumstances I quickly overcame all worries about engaging the Japanese mind in the esoteric details of Reconstruction in the provincial South. They were absorbed from the start.

The second foreign experience was a year at Oxford in their Harmsworth chair of American history. There I was not only confronted with the unflattering mirror of foreign opinion, but with a wave of anti-Americanism brought on by McCarthyism in the circles in which I moved. I knew that my countrymen were better than they sounded—as bad as they undoubtedly did sound. Foreign residence, I find, tends to bring out the latent patriot in me. Now, in the senior common room and high-table conversations at Oxford I felt my face redden occasionally; the sudden hush or change of subject when I was identified, the quick glance over the port or sherry, the sly question put in the inimitable Oxford stammer and bray:

"Professor, Americans spend such incredible sums of money on education. How do you account for the results?"
"Sir, I deplore *any* complacency among my countrymen. In fact I deplore complacency wherever I encounter it."

Though some of my Oxford colleagues knew America well, genuinely shared my concerns about its strident nationalism, and helped me bring my thoughts into focus, they were still foreigners, however friendly, with their own kinds of distortions. I knew that I would never be a Christ Church princeling and would never feel comfortable in a Sorbonne beret. What I needed was native counsel in authentic American accents from a mind I could respect, a mind that shared not only my alarm but my loyalties as well.

Such a mind I found in Reinhold Niebuhr, whose influence I hope I have adequately acknowledged. I did not meet him until after his physical powers were greatly diminished, but I had heard him speak in his prime, and he spoke with the tongue of a prophet and words of fire. He wrote, however, with the calm of a philosopher and the serenity of a learned theologian, and I read him eagerly. Furthermore, he had a grasp on history and he addressed precisely those contemporary American delusions, temptations, and obsessions that absorbed and alarmed me.

Niebuhr located the source of America's ironic plight in the myths of innocence derived from the New England Calvinism and Virginia deism of our national childhood and perpetuated into national adulthood. Now that we had arrived at man's estate we suddenly found ourselves possessed of unprecedented power and wealth and impelled to use this power in ways that inevitably covered us with guilt. In clinging to our infant illusions of innocence along with our newly acquired power, wrote the theologian, we were "involved in ironic perils which compounded the experience of Babylon and Israel"—the perils of overweening power and overweening virtue. These perils gained world significance in finding ironic

105

parallel to some degree in the experience of our opposite number in the world crisis, the USSR. The Russians also, though much more recently, were bred on illusions of innocence and virtue and combined them with Messianic passions that found a lingering reflection in some layers of American conscience and expansionism. Each of these superpowers regarded the other as the embodiment of all wickedness and as the main obstacle to its own plans for bringing happiness to all mankind. Our best course, said Niebuhr, was to put aside our childhood illusions of innocence, along with all self-righteousness, complacency, and humorless idealism, and to face up to the ironic implications of our history.

I derived much insight and support for my ideas from the distinguished theologian. Clearly, his analysis would accommodate my emphasis on the perils of the national myths of success and invincibility, and we were not far apart in what we meant by innocence and the ironic view of our history. All very well. But if I knew that I was not born to the Oxbridge purple or bred to the accent of Paris intellectuals, I also knew that I could claim no authority whatsoever as a theologian. From what authority, then, could I speak in saying some very hard things about American arrogance, complacency, self-righteousness, and intolerance?

The Marxists generally addressed only peripheral aspects of these problems and could claim only a thin residue of collective experience in America. The Muscovite branch was not much given to ironic interpretations of history, and the Soviets were blinded by, among other things, their own ironic counterpart of American innocence. Their American party sought to climb aboard the nationalist bandwagon with their slogan "Communism Is Twentieth Century Americanism." None of these approaches provided me with the authority and detachment I sought as a critic of American nationalism.

The only authority I might claim lay in Southern history, and my strongest personal identity apart from nationality was that of a Southerner. At first this seemed more a handicap than an asset. After all, the South had long been regarded as eccentric and not qualified to speak for the nation in the way that New England or the Middle West could. Furthermore, the South was itself marching to the drums of nationalism, perhaps more in step than anybody else. But the more I thought about the South's past in connection with the nation's present *and* past, the more space and opportunity opened up for detachment, comparison, contrast, and critical perspective. Might I not find a jewel in the toad's head? A source of authority in my own backyard? Instead of Oxford or Paris or Moscow, could it not be found on my native ground?

The South shared a national history with the North, of course, but its experience of the same history was often markedly different, and some of its history was not really shared at all. American history was predominantly a success story, a succession of triumphs over every major historic crisis—economic, political, foreign, or military— with which it had so far been required to cope. This unique record, marred of course by a few serious blemishes passed over or forgotten, left a powerful imprint on the American mind. It bred legends of prosperity, progress, invincibility, righteousness, and innocence. It fostered the national convictions that all American problems had solutions, all American wars ended in victory, and that American purpose and principles would prevail in the end.

The South's claim on these legends and convictions was at best selective, marginal, or vicarious, for its history contained large components of failure, frustration, poverty, moral obloquy, retrogression, defeat, and humiliation not shared by other Americans. If Americans could be described as a people of plenty, Southerners for a century could be more accurately described as a people of poverty. If Americans could believe that all their wars ended in victory, Southerners should somehow have formed a different impression. The South's response to Yankee ideas of human perfectibility, utopianism, and progress and to the notion that all problems had solutions should rightfully be one of skepticism. Skepticism should come as naturally to Southerners as did their deference to elders. As for the illusion of innocence, that would seem to derive small support from centuries of involvement with human bondage and its aftermath. Clearly the South's history was different. The South's distinctive collective experience of the past—not racial policies, economic institutions, or climatic determinants—should be the true source of Southern identity.

Southerners once described themselves as "a peculiar people," and they were indeed set apart by peculiarities within the nation. But looking back over the visitations of misery, invasion, defeat, suffering, and humiliation that most nations have endured, we might wonder if the South's brush with history was all that peculiar. Was it not precisely because of its woes that the South was more typical than peculiar among the peoples of the world? Given the relative immunity from such woes enjoyed by other Americans, was it not *they* who were the "peculiar people"? And was it not those very immunities that helped to breed the illusions, naivetés, impetuosities, and innocence of American nationalism that now frightened both our friends and foes abroad?

With such reflections in mind, I made bold to suggest that the Southern historian might be in a strategic position to help his fellow countrymen understand the ironic implications of their history as well as those of the South's. Admittedly there were obstacles. The history of the South had too often been written defensively, with special pleading in behalf of policies, prejudices, or principles that were parochial in character; and the field had largely been bypassed by the mainstream of national interest.

I took heart, however, from the example set by Southern men of letters. The dawn of the Southern Literary Renaissance, so intoxicating in my youth, was over by then; but several of its leading figures were still productive, and new talents were being discovered every year. Their special challenge to historians, however, was what Allen Tate called "the peculiarly

historical consciousness of the Southern writer" and his production of a "literature conscious of the past in the present."
That plus the literary figures' sharing so many of the historian's values and points of view and, especially, so much of his
subject matter.

The subject matter was not the kind that filled the usual historical novel. Instead the great novelists often wrote about the
obscure, the provincial, the eccentric, the tormented, and the
humble—the uncelebrated. Yet one of those writers had pop-
ulated a single Mississippi county of his own imagining with
characters known throughout the literate world. If obscurity
and provinciality of subject matter proved no obstacle to literature, why should they prove so to history? If Southern novelists, poets, and playwrights could, as Robert Penn Warren
admonished us, "accept the past and its burden" without evasion or defensiveness or special pleading, why should Southern historians not profit from their example? And if they could
break through the veils of myth and illusion that obscured their
own history, might they not help penetrate the legends of success and victory and innocence that obscured the ironic implications of national history?

These reflections found expression in a number of essays
written during the 1950s, some of which, with additions and
revisions, were published in *The Burden of Southern History*
(1960). The title was suggested by the above quotation from
Warren, to whom the book was dedicated. The dedication and
the title could only begin to suggest the influence of the man
and his work and my sense of indebtedness to him. That was
to increase after we became colleagues at Yale a couple of years
later and to deepen during the years that followed. In the latter period the bond, shared by Cleanth Brooks, has been in part
the sort that regularly binds exiles in alien territory. Beyond and
long before that, however, was the appeal of Warren's complex attitudes toward history, the art with which he used history in his poetry and fiction, and his scorn of using it as "a
private alibi-factory" for losers or as a "treasury of virtue" for

winners. In one of his novels he compared the historian with "a scientist fumbling with a tooth and a thigh-bone to reconstruct for a museum some great stupid beast extinct with the ice age." And in *Brother to Dragons* he put in Thomas Jefferson's mouth the question, "What is knowledge without the intrinsic mediation of the heart?"

Two thematic chapters, "The Search for Southern Identity" and "The Irony of Southern History" begin and end the first edition of the *Burden* book, the latter title obviously inspired by Niebuhr's *The Irony of American History* (1952). Between these thematic pieces are chapters, on various historical events and developments scattered over a century, written not so much to advance historical scholarship as to illustrate announced themes. They were intended, of course, to measure up to reasonable scholarly standards on their own. But like written history of other kinds, even that free of thematic and illustrative purpose, these essays were subject to the erosion of time and correction by more recent scholarship.

In a second edition of the book, at the end of a piece entitled "Equality: The Deferred Commitment," I added a "Postscript, 1968," in which I virtually retraced or drastically modified certain important assumptions of the original essay. The essay had traced the evolution of Union war aims from the first, which was strictly limited to preserving the Union, to the second, a more reluctant commitment to emancipation, and finally to the third and most radical war aim of racial equality. Conceding that this last commitment was made piecemeal and with difficulty, I nevertheless maintained that it was a definite commitment and that the Union had reneged on fulfillment for a century. In the "Postscript" I confessed that my own researches and those of other historians had cast serious doubts on the extent of Radical Republican commitment to what I had called "the third war aim," the promise of racial equality. Were I to prepare a third edition of the book, I would doubtless find reason to add postscripts and corrections to other essays, since by this time correction of error and the alteration of viewpoint are neither surprising nor terribly embarrassing. To proceed otherwise would be to write off the ongoing work of historical scholarship as futile.

The subjects of the historical essays were chosen with a view to pointing up the contrast between how the South and the North experienced the same historical event, and to underline Southern experiences, blunders, illusions, and disasters of the past that might have counterparts in the nation's present or future. These included such experiences as trying to define moral rectitude by national or regional boundaries, trying to set up a cordon sanitaire against alien or unorthodox ideas, imposing censorship or coercion to repress freedom of expression, trying to impose one's own institutions or ideology or orthodoxies on one's allies, defending a morally discredited institution, conducting diplomacy with moralistic or legalistic rigidity, relying on economic or military coercion to influence foreign opinion, staking one's whole cause on the defense of one ephemeral economic institution or system, taking for granted that the presumed righteousness of a cause guarantees its ultimate triumph, and forgetting that defeat as well as victory may be a consequence of war. One result of addressing these larger concerns was that in spite of its title the book contains as much about Northern or national history as about Southern.

More literary than historical in subject matter, one of the essays, "A Southern Critique for the Gilded Age," combined an irresistible convenience with an unchallengeable authority. The convenience was that the entire Southern critique of Yankeedom came from the pens of authentically Yankee writers, and the authority lay in the high reputation of three of the most astute critics of their age—Herman Melville, Henry Adams, and Henry James. Each of them—Melville in *Clarel*, Adams in *Democracy*, and James in *The Bostonians*—uses a Southerner, a Confederate veteran, as a mouthpiece for some of the severest strictures on American society voiced in the nineteenth century, though not necessarily the views of the authors.

111

More typical of the historical pieces and more controversial is an essay on John Brown. The emotional, mythic, and divisive nature of the subject presents delicate problems, but there is nothing like John Brown's raid, and the Northern and Southern reactions to it, to illustrate the contrast between sectional experiences of the same event. And few events illustrate so well the consequences of unbridled self-righteousness. "When a noble deed is done, who is likely to appreciate it?" asked Henry David Thoreau, and he answered, "They who are noble themselves."

I shall not attempt to spell out all the historical illustrations and their implications for my thesis. I have already referred to subsequent retractions made in my original interpretation of the Union war aims. Although they blunt the point to some degree, I do not think the modifications dismiss its relevance to the point of fighting wars on borrowed moral capital, then defaulting on the debt, but nevertheless adding its sum to the national "treasury of virtue" and banking on it for futures in moral credit.

I doubt that revisionist scholarship has been more active in any field of American or Southern history than it has in Reconstruction historiography during the last generation. In including an essay on that subject I had in mind lessons for the Second Reconstruction then struggling to be born. Were I revising the essay of the 1950s at the present time, I would make some modifications. But I do not think they would appreciably curtail the implications of the First Reconstruction for the Second Reconstruction that I had in mind. The same is true of any alteration I might make in bringing up to date my treatment of the Populist heritage. The essay on the Civil Rights Movement added later was written in the heat of unfolding events without a needed perspective of time and would now be subject to rather more alterations than otherwise.

After this recapitulation I shall risk exploring the reductionist consequences of the relativist canon of historical criticism. Did the book turn out to share the ephemerality of the circumstances under which it was written? I tried a somewhat premature test of that question with a second edition in 1968. At that time I added an essay of afterthought (not intended as a retraction) called "A Second Look at the Theme of Irony," pointing to two outstanding national issues of the moment to which my thesis might contribute some understanding. These issues were the war in Vietnam and the violent black revolt in Northern cities, both of which seemed to me to suggest that "history has begun to catch up with Americans," that their "fabled immunity from frustration and defeat has faltered," and that their myths of virtue and innocence have "become a stock subject of jeers and ridicule even among our friends" abroad. One characteristic response of Americans was not to abandon their myths but to reaffirm them, and to divide only on which myths they held most inviolable. On Vietnam the hawks clung to invincibility and success, holding defeat or failure unthinkable, while the doves reaffirmed innocence and virtue, finding any increment of guilt intolerable. Both hawks and doves sought to achieve the unachievable at whatever cost, be it for extremists nuclear war on the one hand or unilateral disarmament on the other. Neither was deterred by reference to realism or historical experience. Fortunately many opponents of the war policy were guided by more rational considerations.

On both Vietnam and the black revolt, Americans suddenly found themselves deprived of traditional scapegoats. Foreign misadventures had traditionally been attributed to such imperialists as the British or the French, and the woes and oppressions of black folk were notoriously the responsibility of the South and slavery. Such twinges of conscience as were felt over these matters were conveniently discharged in moralistic denuciations of *European* imperialists and *Southern* racists. But now, whoever was responsible for the Vietnam quagmire, it had undeniably become an *American* war. And wherever the blacks came from, it was mainly *Northern* cities they were burning and Northern policies they were protest-

113

ing. It did seem as if history was at last about to catch up with Americans, and it was doubtful that they could much longer find refuge in their peculiar legends and myths.

On the whole I felt that some central theses of *The Burden* had held up pretty well in the preliminary assessment. And they had held up, I felt, even though history had played an ironic prank on the ironist by placing one Southerner in the White House, a second in the State Department (and, I might have added, a third in command in Vietnam) during the last stand for national legends just described. But then, politicians of Southern origins in high offices, always conscious of the regional incubus on their backs, would be the last to risk offending national sensibilities and the first to pay homage to national myths. My reflections on the South's un-American experience with history were never intended as a policy paper, but I hoped they might have their uses in the shaping of a people's conscience and awareness.

So much for the preliminary test. But now, eighteen years after the 1968 revision, *The Burden* faces a second trial. The plea of double jeopardy is unavailing, and there is no statute of limitation applying to the offenses of historians in pursuit of their craft. Their culpability lasts as long as they are read—and sometimes longer. Let the trial proceed.

In the meantime, much water has flowed under the bridge. America at last had lost a war, suffered an acknowledged defeat, and admitted some lack of righteousness in its prosecution. And simultaneously the nation was made to face gross and impeachable lawlessness in its highest offices. So traumatic were these shocks that for some years it would seem that the country was about to abandon its cherished myths and face up to the irony of its history. The symptoms were striking and they were expressed in sudden waves of cynicism, self-doubt, and above all a spreading conviction of national guilt—a complete reversal, to all appearances, from the old credo of success and innocence. A great market for American guilt opened up temporarily to supply the demand. It was collective guilt the buyers sought, guilt inexpiable and probably ineradicable, guilt incurred over the long past, from the first settlers down to the present. A malaise seemed to sap national self-righteousness, self-confidence, and complacency.

Watching these remarkable developments, I began to wonder if obsolescence had not at last caught up with *The Burden* and if its generation-old thesis had not proved ephemeral after all—as the relativists predicted. Nothing lasts forever, and perhaps its time had come.

Then with the 1980s came a shift in the national mood that was almost as sudden as the arrival of the one that preceded it, and the shift went to the opposite extreme. Opinion polls assured us that Americans had made a miraculous recovery from their malaise. Not only was the pulse of self-esteem strong, it pounded with self-righteousness. A fatuous complacency quieted the rigors of guilt, and innocence was restored by fiat.

In the new order, not only were all American wars righteous, but they all ended in victory, and some would hold that nuclear wars might end similarly, assuming acceptance of a few million casualties. No more nonsense about human rights in foreign policy. And no more quibbling about economic sanctions against potential enemies. Our European allies had better shape up and get in line. If unilateral decrees and economic sanctions proved unavailing, the so-called "Agenda for the Eighties" budgeted more and more and more nuclear missiles. An aggressive foreign policy and bold commitments around the world suggested that the national conscience was preparing to take on new and unprecedented burdens.

On the domestic front the poor, the unemployed, the black people, the young, the aged, and the afflicted were instructed to look to their own resources. Marching orders for the American caravan were to reverse course and retrace its tracks—back over the misguided trail of the Civil Rights Movement, the Great Society, the New Frontier, and the New Deal, back all the way to the golden age of free enterprise a half-century ago.

115

Once there the wagons were to form a circle to defend the old faith in success, invincibility, righteousness, and innocence.

Perhaps, then, we Americans remained a peculiar people after all, or at least retained our yearnings for a faith bred of a very peculiar historical experience. If so, perhaps we might still profit from reflection on the experience of some of our own countrymen upon an encounter with history that was somewhat different from this peculiar success story, yet was rather more typical of that which commonly befalls mankind.

Before taking leave of these reflections on the distinctiveness of the South's encounter with history and the lessons implicit in its experience both for the South itself and for the nation, I feel obliged to admit certain vulnerabilities in the argument. Critics have already pointed out some of them. Aware of them myself from the start, I attempted—but without entire success it would seem—to guard against them. Briefly put, the most vulnerable point lies in the South's response, or lack of it, to its distinctive experience. If the South's experience of history offered so many striking contrasts to the national experience of success, victory, righteousness, opulence, innocence, and overweening power, why has the South not profited more from its experience? Why has it gained so little immunity from national myths of progress, invincibility, and innocence? Why has it so often proved to be the most nationalistic part of the country?

There is plenty of evidence to justify such questions. To turn first to the most blatant instance, the South gloried in polling the largest percentage of the white vote received in the entire country in 1984 for a presidential candidate who staged the most nationalistic campaign for more than a century. He rang all the changes on the old myths. Nor was there any real reason, considering the region's record over the last century from Vietnam back through the Spanish American War and beyond, for surprise over this latest regional embarrassment. As one of my critics, Gaines M. Foster, has observed, in the Filipino rebellion against American imperialists Southern troops "helped to quell the rebels with a rebel yell and displayed no apparent appreciation of the irony."

It was not that I was unaware of these secondary ironies and the consequent vulnerabilities of my argument. In fact I mentioned "the headlong precipitancy with which the South has responded to the slogans of nationalism in recent world crises." My strategy of defense was to switch from the indicative to the subjunctive mood. The indicative, of course, declares a fact, while the subjunctive suggests a possibility, a desire, an admonition, an exhortation: "If it be rightly perceived . . ." "Were their heritage a guide . . ." "Should they take thought . . ." Not that Southerners or historians or Americans *did*, but that they *might* or *could* or *should* or *may* or *must*. The hypothetical, the contingent. It was certainly never my purpose to claim that Southerners were endowed with a special wisdom or had become "a race of philosophers," though I thought a few Southern writers bore evidence of their heritage. With all that in mind I sought consciously to stick to the subjunctive mood in all generalizations about the lessons of Southern history. If I failed to do so consistently it was a slip. When I wrote that the South "had learned," my intended meaning was "had experienced." Since I made it perfectly obvious, however, that I wished very much the South had learned to *apply* the lessons its experience taught, that may have seemed to some to translate the subjunctive into the indicative mood. Richard H. King illustrates both the error and its correction. "As a prescription, it was eloquent and valuable," he writes. "But as history, it made little or no sense." But it was intended as prescription, and as he puts it, "expressed hope for what Southerners might come to believe in the future."

A wider door to misunderstanding was probably opened by the treatment of Southern identity and distinctiveness. Admitting that a deluge of change had swept the South, but rejecting the myths of agrarianism and the racial dogmas offered to maintain its identity, I sought some means by which the South could avoid "the threat of becoming 'indistinguishable,'

117

of being submerged under a national steamroller." All I could offer was "the collective experience of the Southern people . . . their unique historic experience as Americans." Now regional identity, like national character, is normally not something contingent or hypothetical but rather something already possessed in marked and recognizable degree.

Yet in presenting the South's historic heritage as a key to regional distinctiveness and identity, I was proposing, suggesting, sometimes urging a concept, not asserting or claiming a fait accompli. Again the mood was subjunctive, not indicative. The title read, "The *Search* for Southern Identity," not its establishment. To Southerners I said (with emphasis added here), *"it would seem to be* a part of their heritage worth cherishing"; that the Southerner *"should be secure enough* also not to deny a regional heritage because it is at variance with national myth"; and to other Americans that there was "still a contribution *to be derived* from the South's un-American adventure in feudal fantasy." With these rhetorical precautions plus the concession that in spite of its heritage the South still responded "headlong" to nationalist myths it shared only vicariously (the essence of the irony), I had hoped that I might be spared the misunderstandings I sought to avoid.

Quite apart from misunderstandings, those concepts are subject to the more common and inevitable agents of infirmity and decrepitude—those consequent on the passage of time. One of them was suggested earlier in a quotation from Ibsen about the short life-span of regularly constituted ideas—which, of course, the notions under review have long since exceeded. But in addition, time takes another toll on ideas that historians are wont to base upon past experience. As time puts ever-increasing distance between the present and those momentous events of the past, the ideas tied to them tend to dim and fade among later generations—unless they happen to be Irish, or Polish, or others who are able or compelled to live perpetually with the past.

Perhaps we are faced here with a plight common to many of

the teachings of historians and their lessons of the past the threat of a built-in obsolescence, the toll taken by the passage of time. But these only increase the difficulties of the historian; they do not destroy the validity of history. Nor do they necessarily invalidate the wisdom that might, or could, or may, or should be earned or learned from distinctive historical experience.

Chapter 7

Comparing Comparisons

I T WAS NOT that the South was embarrassed for lack of comparative perspective, or its history for lack of a comparative dimension. In fact the South has, if anything, been plagued by comparisons and its history distorted by them. The trouble lay in the comparative partner with which the South was long stuck, namely the North.

Given the geographical and political circumstances of nineteenth-century America, the coupling of North and South in comparisions was more or less inevitable. To both it seemed natural, even unavoidable. They had grown up together, sibling offspring of the same mother country, sharing the same history, the same wars for independence and expansion, the same national allegiance. Isolated geographically from national rivals that normally provide comparative reference and isolated historically as "the first new nation," the first to break away from colonial status, and therefore lacking normal comparative partners in the formative years, Americans turned in upon themselves for comparative reference. Of course *The*

Federalist Papers are a treasure house of comparisons, but they are eighteenth-century documents by former subjects of an empire.

Introversion of the comparative impulse was fostered by the sectional quarrels that broke out between North and South early in the nineteenth century. As I have pointed out elsewhere, the two sections "have served each other as inexhaustible objects of invidious comparison in the old game of regional polemics. *Our* faults are as nothing, they have said over and over again, compared with *theirs*. Compare our candor with their hypocrisy, our forthrightness with their evasiveness." On and on it went, but as it intensified the South tended to assume the burden of proof, to regard itself as distinctive and different, "a peculiar people." Exceptionalism was then seen as a Southern phenomenon, which tacitly—and perhaps unconsciously—brought the North to be regarded as the norm, the mainstream from which an eccentric and peculiar South departed and differed.

That assumption, however, overlooked striking developments in the North that set in about the same time the sectional quarrels began to intensify. The developments in the North were those loosely embraced in the term *modernization* and included urbanization, industrialization, and mechanization. While those changes went forward apace, the antebellum South changed comparatively little, clinging to its rural, agricultural, labor-intensive economy and its traditional folk culture. Looking at the problem in this fashion, James M. McPherson has suggested a reversal of the antebellum perception of sectional roles, making the North instead of the South the deviant from the mainstream of history, the region that became different, the center of national exceptionalism.

Emphasizing the postbellum experience, I had suggested, as McPherson points out, that exceptionalism and distinctiveness of the North had been enhanced by the Civil War and by subsequent experiences that fostered the myth of invincibility, success, opulence, and innocence. These were legends to which the South's experience offered her no genuine entitlement. Indeed, apart from the North, it would be difficult to find any other people of the world whose history might encourage comparable myths or provide much ground for comprehending them. If there were a peculiar people, they might most likely be found above rather than below the Potomac. All in all, the North seemed an unsuitable partner for the South to be coupled with in the comparative study of history. As E. L. Godkin of the *Nation* put it with some exaggeration in 1880 the South "differs nearly as much from the North as Ireland does, or Hungary or Turkey."

Although doubtful of the fruitfulness of traditional North-South comparisons, I nevertheless remained persuaded that the history of both regions and of the nation as a whole stood in great need of comparative dimensions if suitable comparative partners could be found. The tradition of interregional comparison, following old patterns of sectional polemics, had mainly served to perpetuate stale provincialities and outdated quarrels. A raising of comparative consciousness and horizons would surely help to free our history from the isolation in which it was habitually written. Comparison offers possibility of redefining traditional problems, revealing what needs explanation, shaping fresh periodization, discovering unsuspected relationships, proving what seemed ordinary to be rare or unique and what was assumed exceptional to be quite common. It uncovers surprises and varieties and, as Raymond Grew has said, "wins some freedom from the tyranny of what happened and develops that awareness of alternatives . . . that underlies some of the most provocative of historical questions."

In my own writings I had, in a limited and sporadic fashion, ventured comparisons that seemed to be worth pursuing: the First Reconstruction with the Second, for example, or the Cold War of the 1950s with that of the 1850s, and the age of free security with that of insecurity in America. Others have observed that historians, consciously sometimes but mainly unconsciously, are engaged in comparative reference all the time and that nearly all historical judgments, generalizations, and statements are implicitly or explicitly comparative. Would the discipline not profit from a more conscious, considered, and systematic approach to a device so commonly employed?

With these preoccupations in mind, I undertook as editor and contributor the production of a volume of essays entitled *The Comparative Approach to American History* (1968). The twenty-two contributors, apart from the editor, were chosen mainly for their eminence in a particular field of history rather than for their demonstrated talents in the comparative approach. Some of them had displayed such talents and interest, but the majority had not. My fond hope was that a genius for history would evoke untapped gifts for comparative insight. Knowing there was little point in trying to tell such individuals what to do or how to do it, I laid down no rules, prescribed no method, and hoped for the best. The intended audience was the intelligent general reader rather than the professional historian. What I had in mind was similar to what I think Raymond Grew meant when he later wrote, "To call for comparison is to call for a kind of attitude—open, questioning, searching. . . . To call for comparison, however, says almost nothing about how to do this well." The permissiveness proposed is suggested in the introductory essay to that book, in which I say that "comparative reference can illuminate a discussion after the manner of an imaginative and disciplined use of simile, metaphor, or analogy. As in literary usage, the spirit of play is not without relevance in such exercises." In mentioning play, of course, I had no intention of making light of the endeavor. Anyone who has watched people fully engaged in play will realize that it can be one of the most serious of adult employments.

The results were predictably mixed. Masters of their various fields from the colonial period to the Cold War, the distinguished contributors could be depended on to have something interesting to say. Some said it brilliantly and some more readably than others, but the component of comparative insight varied widely from one essay to another. It ranged from full and imaginative engagement with fresh and illuminating perceptions on through mere juxtapositions that left the real work of comparison up to the reader and included a few that did not embrace any clearly comparative dimension at all or made only token gestures. This unevenness was less surprising than was the generally favorable reception the volume received from critics. Exceptions among the latter were those with social-science leanings who deplored the absence of scientific and interdisciplinary methods and techniques of quantification, and from whom, incidentally, applause had not really been expected.

The book was not, of course, a fair test or sample of the comparative approach. For one thing the space allowed contributors was too cramped, and for another there had not been held, as there should have been, a preparatory conference of the authors. I nevertheless hoped that the effort might help to move the guild toward comparative study or at least make its members more tolerant of such deviations. While I should like to believe these hopes were not entirely misplaced, I would not for a moment think of crediting that book with the outburst of comparative activity that took place among American historians in the following years. In the first place signs of this movement had appeared prior to the book's publication, and many other influences contributed to its growth later on.

For my own work, *The Comparative Approach* book was one of several preoccupations encouraging the idea that the South offered special opportunities for and inducements to comparative study not available in the same degree to other fields of American history and other parts of the country. The exceptionalism that the nation boasted and that its nationalist myths celebrated set it apart in several respects from the historical experiences of other nations. I have already suggested why this made the South a poor comparative partner for the North. But the very misfortunes of the South's history that accounted for its inappropriateness as a partner of comparison for the North opened doors to many comparative partners of the world that were closed or limited to the country as a whole.

It was not only the misfortunes such as invasion, devastation, defeat, military occupation, colonial status, and poverty so common throughout the world that facilitated the South's comparability and multiplied its potential partners. Closer home was the character of the economics, demographics, Afro-American populations, and hierarchical societies that were common to the South and to republics below the border. The South held the largest and most conspicuous place in the vast plantation culture that extended from Barbados westward through the Caribbean and on across the continent through Texas, and southward from Virginia and Maryland down across the equator through Brazil and Argentina. Plantation America was, as Charles Wagley called it, "a magnificent laboratory for the comparative approach." All these societies offered the South comparisons of long-term experience with African slavery and other types of forced labor, with plantation life in great variety, with patriarchal family life, planter hierarchies, caste systems, emancipations, reconstructions, and multiple experiments in race relations.

Opportunities of this sort were too tempting to be resisted. The subjects were so large and rich as to inspire ambitions of book proportions. My experiments in them, however, were confined to extended essays, some of which were first published in *American Counterpoint: Slavery and Racism in the North-South Dialogue* (1971). Long predating these efforts was the pioneer work of Frank Tannenbaum, *Slave and Citizen: The Negro in the Americas* (1946), a comparative study with a powerful moral impact. That comparison of the Anglo-American, Protestant, capitalist type of slavery with the Latin-American, Catholic, monarchist type resulted in a terrible indictment of the former. Whereas in the northern continent slavery went unrestrained by church or state or tradition, denied the slave a moral or human status and left its victims crippled in mind, spirit, and personality, slavery in Latin America, according to Tannenbaum's view, was restrained and humanized by church and crown and resulted in racial harmony, tolerance, ethnic mobility, and felicitous assimilation.

Like the Turner frontier thesis, as Peter Kolchin has observed, the Tannenbaum thesis was a challenge, a hypothesis to be tested by further study. In "Protestant Slavery in a Catholic World," I turned to Brazil as a case in point. With the aid of insights provided by new scholarship from and about Brazil, I undertook a critical examination of the work of Gilberto Freyre, the distinguished Brazilian historian who bore chief responsibility for the high reputation his country had come to enjoy for its record in slavery and race relations. While no apologist for slavery, Freyre did maintain that it was more humane, less cruel, and more benevolent in Brazil than it was elsewhere and that race relations there were much more amicable. His own evidence, however, scrutinized in the light of later scholarship called in question his conclusions. This left Brazil a legitimate and illuminating comparative partner for the South in both slavery and race relations, but sharply diminished the invidious conclusions advanced by Freyre.

A subject that opened a door of comparison between the history of the South and the history of all the other slave societies of the New World was the neglected field of Afro-American demography. An important new key to that door was Philip D. Curtin's *The Atlantic Slave Trade: A Census* (1969), a statistical study that corrected the wildly exaggerated estimates of slaves imported from Africa and the proportions of the total received by the various countries and colonies importing them. Since the Southern states had far more slaves than any other slave power, more than all the other slave powers combined at any time in the last twenty-five years of American slavery, it was assumed that their imports from Africa must have been proportional to their enormous slave population. Curtin's study, however, revealed that the British continental colonies and the United States, including French and Spanish territories acquired later, had from the beginning to 1861 imported only 427,000 or 4.5 percent of the total number of Africans brought to the New World by the Atlantic slave trade. Yet by the time of emancipation, the blacks had multiplied more than tenfold in the United States to more than 4 million slaves plus half a million free Afro-Americans.

Nothing remotely comparable occurred in any other of the countries or colonies that together accounted for 95.5 percent of the total imports. In no other slave society, in fact, did the number surviving at the end of slavery come near equaling the number originally imported, and in most they were far fewer. For example, the British West Indies imported 1,665,000 slaves over the centuries, but abolition left a population of only 781,000. The French islands of Martinique and Guadaloupe took in 656,600 but found fewer than a third that number to liberate, and the Dutch colonies with half a million imports counted no more than 20 percent of that total at the end of slavery.

"What is the explanation of this startling marvel?" the abolitionist Robert Dale Owen had asked in 1864. He had pronounced it "marvelous beyond all human preconception." The problems of finding an acceptable explanation for the unique increase of African slave population in America were numerous and complicated enough to keep task forces of comparative historians at work for generations. The task was comparative because every hypothesis involved reference to experience elsewhere. It was complicated because of the almost infinite number of variables involved in each comparison. The most I could hope to do at this juncture was to identify some of the more likely hypotheses, point to the more promising and warn of less plausible ones. They ranged all the way from the antebellum polemical propaganda extremes of benevolent paternalism on the one side to the most hideous form of commercial slave-breeding on the other. In between were such variables as ratios between the sexes and between population and land; human and land fertility; birth and death rates; relations between climate, disease, and medicine, and between master and slave; demands of various crops and production on labor; the state of the market; slave treatment, especially of child-bearing women; the feeding, housing, and punishment of slaves; and particularly the crucial question of when the slave trade was closed. I had no answers, only questions. The work was scarcely begun and the prospect all the more exciting for being at that stage.

An even more interesting prospect lay ahead during the period following slavery in the comparative study of emancipations and reconstructions, a field as yet virtually untouched. As I suggested in a paper pointing out these neglected opportunities, there were as many emancipations and reconstructions as there had been slave systems, and presumably as much was to be gained by the comparative study of them as of slavery. In the great age of emancipations and abolition from 1834 to 1888 six imperial powers and two republics, all with possessions in the vast expanse of plantation America, took part in the historic drama ending slavery. In the Latin societies much emancipation preceded abolition, but in the slave states of the South they virtually coincided—both liberation and abolition occurring simultaneously. So it was that of some six million slaves liberated by various acts of abolition in plantation America over the period of half a century, the Southern slave states accounted for about two thirds of the total. This meant about five times the number liberated in the British West Indies in 1834 and about eight times that of Brazil (which had imported eight and a half times as many slaves). The conjunction of abolition and emancipation gave the American experience a uniquely cataclysmic character and dwarfed all others in scale.

Many other peculiarities made the South's experience differ from that of its comparative partners. One was the high ratio of whites to blacks, about two to one over all. Another was the nature of the slave population—the largest of all, but derived from the smallest number of slaves imported; the farthest removed from African origins when freed, and having had the

129

longest period of acculturation; the only large population to move immediately from slavery to freedom without intervening periods of apprenticeship or gradualist stages. And American slaves were not replaced by coolies as they regularly were in the Caribbean, where for example Trinidad and Guiana imported as many Oriental coolies after slavery as the South had imported Africans in its whole history. Another outstanding difference of the South's experience was the terrible war that ended slavery, a war that took almost as many lives as there were slaves liberated in the British West Indies without any bloodshed. Ours was the only slave society that waged a life-and-death struggle over the issue and where the end of slavery might be described as the death of a society rather than the liquidation of an investment.

Of the multitude of possible comparisons between reconstruction experiences, only two can be mentioned. One is in constitutional adjustments. In no other country of plantation America did whites share with black freedmen the range of political power and office that Southern whites were forced to share briefly with their freedmen. Another contrast of reconstructions was in the matter of violence. Violence there certainly was in Southern Reconstruction, but nothing approaching the Caribbean horror of the bloodbath in Jamaica at Morant Bay in 1865. In spite of important distinctiveness in the South's experience of emancipation and Reconstruction, there were as many similarities, for the long legacy of slavery was much the same everywhere. The richest comparative study involves similarities as well as differences. I urged comparative perspective on the ground that there was no excuse for continuing to study in isolation experiences that were common to many societies, even though not significantly that of the North.

The circumstances under which my paper on "Emancipations & Reconstructions: A Comparative Study" originated have some incidental interest. It was originally presented at the XIII International Congress of Historical Sciences, which met in 1970 at Moscow. The Russian historians who commented on the paper took a generally negative view, found little profit in such comparisons, and pronounced the paper another instance of American claims to "exceptionalism." I was gratified, however, by the intervention of a Polish delegate of somewhat doubtful proletarian credentials who, speaking from the floor, eloquently defended the paper and suggested that its comparative approach could profitably be employed in studies of the emancipation and adjustment of Polish and Russian serfs. I recall no response to his proposal from the Russians. Other comment came later on in published criticism from American colleagues, most notably from LaWanda Cox, a knowledgeable critic, who took me to task for the weight of blame I had placed on the Union authorities for the failure of Reconstruction. I thought she was right and had, in fact, anticipated her criticism by modifying the original statement in the Russian publication for a revised American edition.

I found that the comparative perspective not only opened new subjects, but inspired and required revision of earlier works or suggested new solutions to old controversies about them. An example was the debate over the thesis of the Jim Crow book, samples of which Joel Williamson helpfully collected in *The Origins of Segregation* (1968). At this point the debate was stuck tediously on the question of at what point in linear time the system had significantly emerged. More important, it seemed to me, was to find some means of accounting for the change whenever and wherever it occurred. Since this transition in race relations had taken place in other societies as well as the South, it seemed possible that comparisons might help.

Several illuminating comparative studies in the history of race relations in foreign societies had recently appeared. Among them were Pierre L. van den Berghe, *Race and Racism*, focusing on Mexico, Brazil, and South Africa, and Philip Mason, *Prospero's Magic* (1962) and *Patterns of Dominance* (1970), focusing on India, Latin America, and England. I was alerted to comparative possibilities by Mason's citation of my book on the South to illustrate developments in India. Why not reverse the process? Both van den Berghe and Mason found similar patterns common to the countries they studied. The critical point was the shift from the paternalistic to the competitive type of race relations, with much overlapping—the first relying on social distance and the second on physical distance to define status. Paternalistic relations, built on a master-servant model, encourage distant intimacy, friendly personal contact, and pseudotolerance, whereas competitive relations promote rivalry, estrangement, aloofness, and bigotry and substitute physical distance for legal or assured social distances. Since slavery in the South was probably the most paternalistic of the New World slave systems, this may account for the prolonging of paternalistic race relations into the new order, their overlapping and confusion with the competitive type of relations, and the delay in full segregation. Florestan Fernandes, *The Negro in Brazilian Society* (1969), has explained "the myth of Brazilian racial equality" by the perpetuation, after slavery, of paternalism combined with a tradition of dominance-submission that necessitated no segregation but tolerated no real equality. In the light of these comparisons, the debate on American Jim Crow advanced several strides.

Among American historians comparative history, or more broadly comparative consciousness, has taken on new life, with special activity in the fields of slavery, emancipation, reconstruction, and race relations. An early pioneer, Eugene D. Genovese, has expanded his fruitful contributions to this field; David Brion Davis continues his monumental studies of the problem of slavery in the West; Herbert Klein has compared slavery in Virginia and Cuba, and Richard S. Dunn has pressed his comparisons of plantations in Virginia and Jamaica; and Stanley L. Engerman promises light on the puzzle of comparative slave populations. Widening comparative horizons, Carl N. Degler has compared slavery and race relations in Brazil and the United States; Peter Kolchin has compared Russian defenses of serfdom and American proslavery arguments, as well as resistance to bondage in the two countries; and Orlando Patterson has extended comparisons of slavery to "the dawn of human history." Two brilliant comparative studies, one by George M. Fredrickson and one by John W. Cell, of the history of race relations in South Africa and the American South have lent distinction to the list.

These are only a few examples of many that could be named. It will be obvious that they all take off from the problems in Southern history. While comparative work has been done in other fields, for example frontier history, I believe it is fair to say that the greatest number and probably the most successful and stimulating experiments in comparative history of recent years have stemmed from, or been suggested by, questions arising from the history of the South. The authors may, and often do, come from elsewhere, but if their interests take a comparative turn, they seem irresistibly attracted to the riches inherent in the Southern experience and the opportunities it offers for comparison.

Chapter 8

Summing Up Accounts

O VER THE YEARS the offenses and misdemeanors charged against a historian in the practice of his trade can add up to quite a list. Among the charges for which I have been held answerable at various times are those of being a one-time activist, a part-time moralist, a full-time presentist, an addicted ironist, and once even "the ironist as moralist." That amounts to a formidable bill of indictment. Some of these charges I have confessed or demurred to in earlier chapters, and some will receive further attention. One charge, not mentioned above, is more of an ideological classification than an indictable offense. That is the tag of "liberal" with which I was stuck pretty early and have more or less remained encumbered. It has been worn both with pride and also with a certain discomfort that calls for explanation.

In the years of struggle over race relations, starting long before the Civil Rights Movement got underway and continuing through its course, the term *liberal* was all but unavoidable for anyone with my views. Admitting a wide span of differences among those who wore it, the identification was clear enough for the issue at hand and could be worn with honor. I am not about to disavow it in that connection. But the term *liberal* had a longer history and many more uses. Some of those uses remain acceptable enough. Worn by a Southerner, however, the identification drew one into some strange company and implied a heritage that I could never reconcile with my own views of past or present. The postbellum tradition of liberalism in the South originated with the New South school of Henry W. Grady and Richard H. Edmonds and their apostles and came down through Henry Watterson, Walter Hines Page, John Spencer Bassett, and Edwin Mims. Theirs was, in general, a cheerful and optimistic creed of progress, industry, and nationalism. The very few who spoke up for racial justice were also called liberals, but they were a tiny handful on the order of George W. Cable. The rest preached reconciliation of sections, classes, and races—all under proper white rule. They usually revered the Lost Cause and its memory, abhorred Reconstruction and its works, and ignored or deplored the Populists and all their ideas. Hence my discomfort in sharing their label: we usually turned up on opposite sides.

Michael O'Brien was perfectly correct in saying in his critique that my somber view of the past had little appeal for the run of Southern liberals, but he was mistaken in assuming their "euphoric" views were part of my "Burden." He was misled by the common label we were fated to wear. Whether the views of history that I advanced and that Southern liberals found so unattractive were more appealing to conservatives, as he thinks, or to radicals for that matter, would depend on what use, if any at all, either found for them. They were not suggested for partisan uses. Nor do I think history need be written for ideological purposes. Nor would I likely have put forth as a regional consensus what I ventured as original ideas. Nor did I assume that its distinctive historic experience had endowed the South with a special wisdom—only with a potential if largely untapped source of wisdom, as well as a basis of regional identity.

Another label I have been invited to assume, this one as presented by Robert B. Westbrook, is that of "Liberal Realist." If this school is accurately typified by Reinhold Niebuhr and George Kennan, it would certainly be distinguished and attractive company—even though I am courteously segregated as a country cousin, or "a southern variation on an American theme." I have already acknowledged indebtedness to Niebuhr, though I am obliged to reject the suggestion that I have offered Southern history in the place of original sin. And it is too much of a burden to say that I offered it as "a conscience for the nation as a whole." I also think it is stretching a point to say that "Irony is a theme which runs throughout the whole of Woodward's work," though I would readily admit that it informs much of it.

The really troubling thing is the psychological and political consequences attributed to the ironic perception of history and social change. In Richard H. King's view it "becomes a way of avoiding clear judgments." Irony, we are told by others, can erode action, make one "prone to timidity and a paralysis of will," can even "degenerate into bemused detachment." Now no one who ever witnessed Reinhold Niebuhr in full eruption on the stump or at the political podium can have a moment's worry about the devitalizing effects of irony for him. No bemused detachment there! And yet he would probably have agreed that anyone who proposes to enter the study of history in search of truth harboring disdain for the thread of irony had best stay out of the labyrinth.

It is easy to concede that "a myth that depends for its survival upon an accurate rendering of the past" is in trouble, and that to endow such a past "with mythical import is clearly an uphill battle." But that is not to agree that myth-making is what the accurate rendering of the past is about. Rather it seems to me a means of exposing myth and overcoming cultural amnesia, a therapy of anamnesis, though that is surely another uphill battle. If the assignment entrusts historians with "priestly responsibility," they know very well they have served such functions before to less worthy ends.

All this harping on the South and its troubles—its prickly distinctiveness, its un-American experiences, its cherished woes of "ole times there and not forgotten"—on and on. The persistence of the theme, especially in its older and more whiny phases, has tried the patience of some and not gone down well with others. A few of the raised eyebrows deserve acknowledgment. Observers from European countries, particularly those long accustomed to the presence within their borders of minority enclaves quite distinctive in religion, language, or culture, some with long-term separatist impulses, have been puzzled if not impatient with the distinctive place assigned the South in American chronicles and letters, not to mention contemporary thought.

One of America's most knowledgeable, sympathetic, and patient foreign critics was Sir Denis Brogan. He early spotted America's illusions of omnipotence, and he had a penetrating understanding of the South too; but even his patience had its limits. In a rather uncharacteristic essay a few years after the Second World War, suggesting new perspectives the war had brought to our views of the past, he pointedly wondered how long Southerners would continue to complain about starvation during the siege of Vicksburg after the siege of Leningrad, or for that matter the slaughter of Shiloh or Gettysburg after Stalingrad or the Battle of the Bulge, or the ruins of Richmond or Atlanta or Columbia after Dresden or Warsaw or Hiroshima, or the lot of losers and the severities of Reconstruction after the experiences of countries in the Balkans and Eastern Europe. He confessed that he had at times been reminded of the Irish, who still spoke of Cromwell as a contemporary. I am sure Brogan did not have in mind any contribution of my own to such lamentations, for there were none. But in another piece on the interpretation of the Southern past he did wag an accusing finger and find me rather unduly "burdened with the *damnosa hereditas* of the South." That admonition has admittedly prompted some soul-searching.

In his more impersonal admonitions Brogan was only reminding us of the erosions that the passage of time works on self-images, grievances, and convictions based on historic experience—what I have earlier referred to as the built-in obsolescence of the lessons taught by historians. (And here I might concede that in current usage "the South" often refers to hemispheric rather than regional phenomena and that North-South relations commonly means relations between the Third World and the developed nations.) The same sorts of questions have been raised by voices closer home, for example in a gentle aside by Emory M. Thomas. He has no trouble understanding what I have to say or agreeing with much of it, yet he permits himself a smile over "renewed [but unintentional] irony in 'The Irony of Southern History.' " He is certainly justified in pointing out that "times have changed considerably since 1953," that "the South's relation to the rest of the country seems to have changed radically," and that the "time has come to ask new questions about southern experience and identity."

The point about the renewed irony is sufficiently made by the picture of the modern South with its conspicuous and vulgar opulence in some quarters (though by no means in all and certainly not the majority) appearing in the rags of Lazarus to lecture the nation about the region's "long and quite un-American experience with poverty." The historic experience with poverty was real enough, but like some other Southern experiences of the past its impact, its perceived influence was more keenly felt when it was still more widely shared or more vividly remembered than it was to become later.

Although I am quite prepared to make appropriate concessions to the erosion of time and to welcome increase in per capita whatever, I balk at changing the rules and familiar boundaries of the subject in the middle of the game. It has been astonishing, not to say embarrassing, to witness the heedless speed and conformity with which presumably serious-minded Southerners, many historians among them, have taken to mouthing and accepting a tag coined a few years ago by some Yankee journalist—"The Sunbelt." It offends in countless ways.

To begin with meteorological foundations, the South enjoys more inches of rainfall per year than any other region in the country. The more precipitation, the more clouds and the less sun. It could more appropriately be dubbed the Cloudbelt. To link it with the region of lowest rainfall is to dump the Dismal Swamp in with Death Valley. But the more grievous offenses to logic lie in false cultural and historical identifications— Charleston with San Diego, Richmond with Los Angeles, North Carolina with Arizona, South Carolina with New Mexico. The history and culture and politics of the far Southwest have few bonds with the South, and the two regions share even less historical experience and tradition than the South shares with the Northeast. Cotton-and-slavery expansionists of the 1850s once entertained imperialist designs on the arid Southwest, but eventually gave them up as hopeless. Whether the Sunbelt slogan means Southern designs of cultural imperialism on the Southwest or vice versa, the prospects would seem equally unpromising.

This is not to say that the South remains frozen in cultural patterns of the past. Florida, after all, was one of the eleven states of the Confederacy, whatever it has become. And the Florida phenomenon is not confined to the peninsula. Walker Percy has (with a few shudders) imagined for the not-too-distant future a "Southern Rim stretching from coast to coast, an L.A.–Dallas–Atlanta axis . . . an agribusiness–sports–vacation–retirement–'show-biz' culture with its spiritual center perhaps at Oral Roberts University, its media center in Atlanta, its entertainment industry shared by Disney World, the

Superdome, and Hollywood. In this scenario the coastal plain of the old Southeast will be preserved as a kind of museum, much like Williamsburg." Presumably the lessons of history would find a niche in the museum.

Another geological or meteorological metaphor conceivable for the fate of the South is that of a landslide, an avalanche descending from above to overwhelm the Southern landscape and bury its monuments under a cultural debris apron. Geologists tell us that a line lying roughly along the Ohio River marks the southernmost encroachment of the ice cap during the last ice age, thus offering the boldest theorizers a geological hypothesis of regional determinism. What I am referring to here is a demographic phenomenon of social-economic origins already in progress, the flight of people and industries from deteriorating cities and economies of the North, in search of advantage, economic or climatic, in the South. Should that exodus accelerate to the degree threatened, the "Landslide South" could become as culturally nondescript as the jerrybuilt "Sunbelt" horror. The consequences for cultural amnesia and the lessons of history would be equally serious.

It is the suggestion of Walker Percy that the South has already pushed past the decisive historic milestone that marked the end of "the period of the long Southern Obsession." The obsession lasted some 150 years, from the time the region succumbed to the combined temptations of slavery and the cotton gin. So long as it lasted the energies and talents of the South were largely absorbed in the defense of slavery or peonage or caste or segregation or some other abomination. The great question is, "now that the old burden is removed," as Percy puts it, or "now that the obsession is behind us," what will Southerners do with the energies and talents thus released? Free at last, will they come forth with some distinctive contribution, some burst of creativity such as that of the Virginia Dynasty before the Great Obsession settled in? "Or will they simply meld into the great American flux?" It is Percy's hope that

141

at least they "will retain a soupçon of difference," a difference that "might even leaven the lump."

It is an attractive idea, this last suggestion, a possibility not to be casually dismissed. The question remains, however, what prospect exists for retaining that leavening difference, even so much as the soupçon required, in the face of burial under portended or progressing landslides, avalanches, and sundry cultural catastrophes? If the essentially distinguishing difference, identity, whatever we call it, were really defined or determined by the Great Obsession, and if that is now all really behind us, what then? What's left?

But to accept that definition would seem to suggest a return to reliance for regional identity on the old "Central Theme" of white supremacy—"the cardinal test of a Southerner," Ulrich B. Phillips called it—even though this time in a mood of relief or release instead of the old one of fatalism or resolution. In either case it tends to put all our eggs in one basket. That is what the antebellum South did with slavery in the first Lost Cause, the Agrarians on an intellectual level in a second, and the racists on the popular level in a third. Time after time through its history the South has gone through jolting, disruptive discontinuities—among them emancipation, industrialization, and now the end (or temporary subsidence?) of the Obsession. Each time many Southerners rallied to the cause, persuaded that if it were lost all would be lost.

As things turned out in each case there proved to be more to it than the ephemeral cause on which all was said to hang— whether institution, idea, or obsession. They all passed on, adding to the accumulating Old Souths. And with the passing of each some Southerners, even some among the last ditchers, breathed a sigh of relief. It would not seem, then, that any one of the lost causes, even the last and most durable, defined the Southern heritage, explained or captured its distinctiveness, or provided a lasting basis for Southern identity. Rather, the key would seem to lie in the history, the collective experience of the Southern people of all colors. Over the distinctive character and meaning of that experience, historians are obliged to continue their quarrels with each other.

How to justify the dedication of a whole career, or the better part of one, to reflections on these parochial concerns of past and present was another question. It was doubtful that a few contributions dug from archives to illuminate in books and monographs some of the darker and more neglected or mis-construed figures, periods, episodes, and problems of the subject added up to a satisfactory answer. In sessions of silent doubt, memory would flash back across the years to the young apprentice in Chapel Hill bursting out of the stacks in despair and pacing Franklin Street alone in the small hours. What had I got myself into? Wouldn't any conceivable alternative be bet-ter? If it had to be history, why not second-century Rome? Or for that matter the Greeks, where it all happened first? Any-thing but this!

Doubts could be temporarily allayed by such commonplace reflections as the thought that the human dilemmas of history are much the same in any place and period. And after all, as places and periods go, the nineteenth- and twentieth-century South encapsulated quite a lot: power and glory, democracy and slavery, decline and fall, civil war and defeat, emancipa-tion and reconstruction, kaleidoscopic change and furious re-bellion. But all this was not enough to bind me to the subject. Nor were the colorful dramatis personae who crowded the stage from Jefferson to Tom Watson and beyond. It was nei-ther heroes nor villains I was seeking. Nor was I bitten by any ideological bug. And certainly the existing historical literature had not captured my fancy. Though surely something of a challenge, it was, with exceptions, more of a repellent than an attraction.

A subtler discouragement, of which I was then only half aware, was a popular delusion, probably not limited to the South but prevalent there, that to study, teach, and write about the past was to condone, approve, and identify with it. To become a historian was therefore to turn one's back on the present and future and become a member of what Emerson in one of his less brilliant dichotomies called the Party of Memory, as against that of Hope. This meant an endorsement of the status quo, for in the prevailing Southern view, the past was taken to justify, defend, and validate the present order. Historians could find themselves caught in embarrassing embraces under that assumption. So conceived, the history profession was a sort of priesthood, one with vows often spelled out and fully comprehended only after they were taken—if ever. Hence it could be a delayed-action trap for the unwary, though some never realized they had been entrapped, and of course many did not need to be. At least I knew I wanted no part of that.

What did more than anything else, I believe, to overcome these misgivings was the example and work, not of historians, but of contemporary men and women of letters in the South, especially the novelists. They too wrote about the past, the Southern past, or more typically the past in the present. But the best of them clearly labored under no vows to justify or celebrate any past or present they wrote about. They might conjure up the past to illuminate, to explain, or to give meaning to the present, but not to vindicate it. The characters they created betrayed no need for heroes or villains on the part of their creators; and the stories they told were shaped by no creed and illustrated no theory about past, present, or future. Their example did not encourage sociological generalization about types, classes, or races—planters, yeomen, poor whites, or slaves—but rather supported the historian's concern for the particular, the concrete, the individual. Most important of all was the proof so magnificently presented in their work that the provincial subject matter we shared was no trap of obscurity but an embarrassment of riches, a treasure of neglected opportunity.

Sitting down to his task with these assurances in mind, the Southern historian found himself in the company of Warren's Jack Burden, of *All the King's Men*, first while he was poring over the antebellum letters of Cass Mastern, inundated by the facts and baffled by the truth that cost a man's life; then in his second excursion into the past, when he was overwhelmed by the truth he sought to elude that cost his father's life; and in his third, when the facts and truth united in the tragedy that took the life of Willie Stark. Or in the company of Faulkner's Quentin Compson and Shreve McCannon in their cold Harvard room past midnight relentlessly pursuing the mystery of a tragedy that had wiped out the dynasty of Sutpen's Hundred by fratricide, incest, miscegenation, murder, and suicide. In their collaboration, Quentin and Shreve use Colonel Thomas Sutpen (1807–1869) and the character of "innocence" assigned him as a historical hypothesis in their imaginative reconstruction of the past. That plus a few hard facts and surviving documents, along with mouth-to-mouth stories, ill-informed testimony, eye-witness accounts, and much ingenious conjecture, analysis of motives, and logical inference. In addition to being a superb detective story and William Faulkner's finest novel, *Absalom, Absalom!* is a disquisition on how, thinking back, we come to "know" the past.

Accustomed to such company and such wayward deviations from the norm in his calling, a historian who addresses, for example, the history of black people or race relations will likely have in mind not only historical events and persons, but also Faulkner's Lucas Beauchamp, Sam Fathers, Joe Christmas, Dilsey, Charles Bon, Jim Bond, Clytie, and the protagonist of "Pantaloon in Black"—all individuals, not a "type" among them. If planters and their heirs are the subject, General Compson, Old Carothers, Isaac McCaslin, and McCaslin Edmunds will figure in the equation. If the poor whites, how can the Bundrens, their most memorable representatives in print, be kept from mind? If it is operators in the New South style, how can the Snopeses or that defector from the broadcloth, Jason Compson, be put aside entirely?

But this deposition in its literary parts would only seem to add to the already formidable bill of indictment framed by the

145

critics. For it adds to the charges of being a presentist, a moralist, an ironist, and a one-time activist, of being a chronicler with a weakness for history-with-a-purpose and one influenced by a theologian, the still graver charge of being a historian, presumably dedicated to fact, who is inspired by fiction. That poses the question of whether the present deponent testifies for the defense or for the prosecution. The answer, I am afraid, will have to be left to the reader. Further, deponent sayeth not.

A Selective List of Critical Works

In place of footnote citations, the following list should assist the reader in locating works either mentioned in the text or of relevant interest.

Benedict, Michael Les. "Southern Democrats in the Crisis of 1876–1877: A Reconsideration of *Reunion and Reaction.*" *Journal of Southern History*, XLVI (1980), 489–524.

Billings, Dwight B., Jr. *Planters and the Making of a "New South": Class, Politics, and Development in North Carolina, 1865–1900.* Chapel Hill, 1979.

Brogan, Denis. "David M. Potter." In *Pastmasters: Some Essays on American Historians*, edited by Marcus Cunliffe and Robin W. Winks. New York, 1968.

———. "The Impending Crisis of the Deep South." *Harper's Magazine* (April, 1965), 147–51.

Carlton, David. *Mill and Town in South Carolina, 1880–1920.* Baton Rouge, 1982.

Carter, Dan T. "From the Old South to the New: Another Look at the Theme of Change and Continuity." In *From the Old South to the New: Essays on the Transitional South*, edited by Walter J. Frazer, Jr., and

List of Critical Works

Winfred B. Moore, Jr., Westport, Conn., 1981.

Cell, John W. *The Highest Stage of White Supremacy: The Origins of Segregation in South Africa and the American South.* Cambridge, 1982.

Clayton, Bruce. *The Savage Ideal: Intolerance and Intellectual Leadership in the South, 1890–1914.* Baltimore, 1972.

Cooper, William J., Jr. *The Conservative Regime: South Carolina, 1877–1890.* Baltimore, 1968.

Cotterill, Robert S. "The Old South to the New." *Journal of Southern History*, XV (February, 1949), 3–8.

Cox, La Wanda. *Lincoln and Black Freedom: A Study in Presidential Leadership.* Columbia, S.C., 1981.

Crowe, Charles. "Tom Watson, Populists, and Blacks Reconsidered." *Journal of Negro History*, LX (1970), 99–116.

Davenport, F. Garvin, Jr. *The Myth of Southern History: Historical Consciousness in Twentieth-Century Southern Literature.* Nashville, 1970.

Degler, Carl N. *Place Over Time: The Continuity of Southern Distinctiveness.* Baton Rouge, 1977.

————. *The Other South: Southern Dissenters in the Nineteenth Century.* New York, 1974.

Fields, Barbara. *Slavery and Freedom in the Middle Ground.* New Haven, 1985.

Foster, Gaines M. "Woodward and Southern Identity." *Southern Review*, XXI (Spring, 1985), 351–60.

Friedman, Lawrence J. *The White Savage: Racial Fantasies in the Postbellum South.* Englewood Cliffs, N.J., 1970.

Gaston, Paul M. "C. Vann Woodward, Southern Historian." *Virginia Quarterly Review* (Spring, 1983), 327–34.

Genovese, Eugene D. "Potter and Woodward on the South." In Eugene Genovese, *In Red and Black: Marxian Explorations in Southern and Afro-American History.* New York, 1971.

Goodwyn, Lawrence. *Democratic Promise: The Populist Movement in America.* New York, 1976.

Green, James R. "Rewriting Southern History: An Interview with C. Vann Woodward." *Southern Exposure*, XII (November-December, 1984), 87–92.

Grew, Raymond. "The Case for Comparing Histories." *American Historical Review*, LXXXV (October, 1980), 763–78.

Hackney, Sheldon. "Origins of the New South in Retrospect." *Journal of Southern History*, XXXVIII (May, 1972), 191–216.

Hahn, Steven. *The Roots of Southern Populism: Yeoman Farmers and the*

A Selective List of Critical Works

Transformation of the Georgia Upcountry, 1850–1890. New York, 1983.

Harris, Carl V. "Right Fork or Left Fork? The Section-Party Alignments of Southern Democrats in Congress, 1873–1897." *Journal of Southern History,* XLII (November, 1976), 471–506.

King, Richard H. "The New Southern Liberalism: V. O. Key, C. Vann Woodward, Robert Penn Warren." In Richard H. King, *A Southern Renaissance: The Cultural Awakening of the American South, 1930–1955.*

Kolchin, Peter. "In Defense of Servitude: American Proslavery and Russian Proserfdom Arguments, 1760–1860." *American Historical Review,* LXXXV (October, 1980), 809–827.

Kousser, J. Morgan. *The Shaping of Southern Politics: Suffrage Restrictions and the Establishment of the One-Party South, 1880–1910.* New Haven, 1974.

——— and James M. McPherson, eds. *Region, Race, and Reconstruction: Essays in Honor of C. Vann Woodward.* New York, 1982.

McPherson, James M. "Antebellum Southern Exceptionalism: A New Look at an Old Question." *Civil War History,* XXIX (September, 1983), 230–44.

McWhiney, Grady. "Continuity in Celtic Warfare." *Continuity: A Journal of History,* I (Spring, 1981), 1–17.

Meier, August, and Elliott Rudwick. "A Strange Chapter in the Career of Jim Crow." In *The Making of Black America: Essays in Negro Life and History,* edited by August Meier and Elliott Rudwick. 2 vols. New York, 1969. Volume II.

Moore, James Tice. "Redeemers Reconsidered: Change and Continuity in the Democratic South, 1870–1900." *Journal of Southern History,* XLIV (August, 1978), 357–78.

O'Brien, Michael. "C. Vann Woodward and the Burden of Southern Liberalism." *American Historical Review,* LXXVIII (June, 1973), 589–604.

Parker, William N., ed. "The Structure of the Cotton Economy of the Antebellum South." *Agricultural History,* XLIV (January, 1970), 1–165.

Patterson, Orlando. *Slavery and Social Death: A Comparative Study.* Cambridge, Mass., 1982.

Percy, Walker. "Random Thoughts on Southern Literature, Southern Politics, and the American Future." *Georgia Review,* XXXII (1979), 499–511.

Perman, Michael. *The Road to Redemption: Southern Politics, 1869–1879.* Chapel Hill, 1984.

A Selective List of Critical Works

Peskin, Allan. "Was There a Compromise of 1877?" *Journal of American History*, LX (June, 1973), 63–75.
Polakoff, Keith Ian. *The Politics of Inertia: The Election of 1876 and the End of Reconstruction*. Baton Rouge, 1973.
Potter, David M. "C. Vann Woodward." In *Pastmasters: Some Essays on American Historians*, edited by Marcus Cunliffe and Robin W. Winks. New York, 1969.
Rabinowitz, Howard N. *Race Relations in the Urban South, 1865–1890*. New York, 1978.
Rable, George C. "Southern Interests and the Election of 1876: A Reappraisal." *Civil War History*, XXVI (1980), 347–61.
Roper, John H. "C. Vann Woodward's Early Career—The Historian as Dissident Youth." *Georgia Historical Quarterly*, LXIV (1980), 7–21.
Saunders, Robert. "Southern Populists and the Negro, 1893–1895." *Journal of Negro History*, LIV (1969), 240–61.
————. "The Transformation of Tom Watson, 1894–1895." *Georgia Historical Quarterly*, LIV (1970), 339–56.
Seip, Terry L. *The South Returns to Congress: Men, Economic Measures, and Intersectional Relationships, 1868–1879*. Baton Rouge, 1983.
Sharkey, Robert P. *Money, Class, & Party: An Economic Study of Civil War and Reconstruction*. Baltimore, 1959.
Shaw, Barton C. *The Wool-Hat Boys: Georgia's Populist Party*. Baton Rouge, 1984.
Thomas, Emory M. "The Paradoxes of Confederate Historiography." In *The Southern Enigma: Essays on Race, Class, and Folk Culture*, edited by Walter L. Fraser, Jr., and Winfred B. Moore, Jr., Westport, Conn., 1983.
Tindall, George B. *The Persistent Tradition in New South Politics*. Baton Rouge, 1975.
Wayne, Michael. *The Reshaping of Plantation Society: The Natchez District, 1860–1880*. Baton Rouge, 1983.
Westbrook, Robert B. "C. Vann Woodward: The Southerner as Liberal Realist." *South Atlantic Quarterly*, LXXVII (1978), 54–71.
Wiener, Jonathan M. *Social Origins of the New South: Alabama, 1860–1885*. Baton Rouge, 1978.
————. "Class Structure and Economic Development in the American South, 1865–1955." *American Historical Review*, LXXXIV (October, 1979), 970–92.

Williamson, Joel. *The Crucible of Race: Black-White Relations in the American South Since Reconstruction.* New York, 1984.
————, ed. *The Origins of Segregation.* Boston, 1968.
Woodman, Harold D. "Economic Reconstruction: Change and Continuity in the Postbellum Era." A paper read at the 1983 meeting of the Organization of American Historians.
Wright, Gavin. *The Political Economy of the Cotton South: Households, Markets, and Wealth in the Nineteenth Century.* New York, 1978.
Wyatt-Brown, Bertram. "W. J. Cash and Southern Culture." In *From the Old South to the New: Essays on the Transitional South,* edited by Walter J. Fraser, Jr., and Winfred B. Moore, Jr. Westport, Conn., 1981.
Zinn, Howard. *The Southern Mystique.* New York, 1964.

Index

153

Index

Brogan, Sir Denis, 138–39
Brooks, Cleanth, 109
Brown, John, 112
Brown v. Board of Education of Topeka: decision of, 68; response to, 83–84; and NAACP brief, 88–89; massive resistance to, 90–91
Bruce, Philip Alexander, 25
Buck, Paul H., 26
Burden of Southern History: and national mood of 1950s, 101–103; and Southern nationalism, 103; Tokyo experience and, 104; Oxford and, 104–105; Niebuhr's influence in, 105–106; Southern distinctiveness and, 107; Warren's influence, 109; correcting errors in, 110–11; 1968 revision of, 114; tested for obsolescence, 115; critics and vulnerabilities of, 116–18; subjunctive mood in, 117–19
Byrd, Senator Harry F., 90

Caldwell, Erskine, 12
Carlton, David, 78
Cash, Wilbur J.: on savage ideal, 15; as voice of Southern consensus, 27; on continuity of New with Old South, 63; as bible of neo-continuitarians, 72, 77; mentioned, 68
Cell, John W., 97, 133
Celts, 71–72
Central Pacific Railroad, 49
Chapel Hill, North Carolina, 17–19, 22–27
Charles II of England, 71
Chaucer, Geoffrey, quoted, 2
Citizens' Councils, 90
Civil Rights Act of 1964, pp. 68, 70, 92
Civil Rights Movement, 112, 115, 135
Civil War, 52, 76–79
Coles, Robert, 35
Colonial economy, 66
Colquitt, Alfred H., 74
Columbia University: graduate work at, 21, 85; teaching at, 41

Commager, Henry Steele, 52
Commission on Interracial Cooperation, 85
Comparative Approach to American History: preoccupations of, 121–23; contributors to, 124; appraisal of, 125
Compromise of 1877: old account of, 47–49; covert aspects of, 50; important parts fulfilled, 53; as most durable compromise, 53
Confederate States: Freeman on, 24; worthies of, 31; ephemerality of, 59–60
Contempo, 18
Continuity, of New South politics, 75; and South's distinctiveness, 75; and *Origins*, 78
Continuity, 70, 71
Convict leasing, 64, 71
Cooper, William J., Jr., 70
Cotterill, Robert S., 63, 68
Couch, William T., 17, 18–19
Cox, La Wanda, 131
Critics, 4–6
Cromwell, Oliver, 138
Curtin, Philip D., 127–28

Davis, David B., 132
Dawson, Francis W., 71
Debs, Eugene V., 43–44
Degler, Carl N.: on continuity and distinctiveness of South, 75–76; on slavery and Civil War, 76–77; on comparative slavery, 132; mentioned, 79
Depression: of 1930s, in South, 9–14 *passim*; of 1890s, 37
Detroit, 92
Dew, Charles B., 67
Du Bois, W. E. B., 24, 86
Dunn, Richard S., 132
Dunning, William A., 24

Edmunds, Richard H., 77, 136
Emancipation. *See* Abolition
Emerson, Ralph Waldo, 144
Emory University, 19, 21, 85

Index

Index

Potter, David M.: on Southern mentality, 15; as fellow student, 21; on *Tom Watson*, 35; on *Reunion*, 52; conversations with, 94
Progressivism, 75
Prussian Road, 72–73

Rabinowitz, Howard, 96–97
Race relations, 90–91, 131–33
Ramsdell, Charles, 44
Raper, Arthur, 85
Reconciliation, 26, 65
Reconstruction: historians of, 24; economic forces in, 56; works on, 59–60; popular image of, 61–62; compared with Redemption, 64; and Second Reconstruction, 92, 112, 123; Japanese fascinated by, 104; revisionists on, 112; comparative studies of, 129–31
Redding, J. Saunders, 85
Redemption: image of, 62; as restoration, 62; leaders and policies of, 64–65; conservative defense of, 71
Reunion and Reaction: as an unanticipated book, 47, 49, 51; traditional story of, 48–49; as jigsaw puzzle, 49; as detective work, 50–52; initial reception of, 52; delayed criticism of, 53–55; additional criticisms by author, 55–57; cautionary qualifications, 54–55. *See also* Compromise of 1877

Sayers, Dorothy, 52
Scott, Thomas A., 49
Scottsboro case, 86
Segregation: viewed as unalterable, 87; role of law in, 96; exclusion and, 96; and black nationalism, 98; origins of, 131
Seip, Terry L., 54–55
Selma march, 91
Sharkey, Robert, 56, 69
Shaw, Barton C., 39
Simkins, Francis B., 24

Slavery: comparative study of, 126–27, 132–33; in the Americas, 128–29; uniqueness of Southern, 130
South Africa, 97
South Carolina, 70–71, 78
Southern Conference on Human Welfare, 19
Southern Historical Association, 63, 89–90
Southern Pacific Railroad, 49
Southern Renaissance: in early 1930s, 9; excitement of, 23; historical consciousness in, 108–109
Soviet Union, 103, 106
Spanish American War, 116
Stein, Gertrude, 18
Stephens, Alexander H., 61
Stevenson, Robert Louis, 33
Strange Career of Jim Crow: origins of, 81–82; thesis of, 82–83; foreign experiences and, 87–88; sales of, 90, 93; Martin Luther King on, 92; misreadings of, 93; presentism in, 94, 95; response to criticisms of, 95–98; reflections on writing of, 98–99. *See also* Segregation
Sunbelt, current usage of term, 140

Tacitus, 8
Tannenbaum, Frank, 126–27
Tate, Allen, 18, 108–109
Thomas, Emory M., 139
Thompson, Holland, 25
Thucydides, 6
Tilden, Samuel J., 53
Tindall, George, 13, 75
Tocqueville, Alexis de, 15
Tokyo, University of, 104
Tom Watson: Agrarian Rebel: origins of, 20; opportunities offered by, 31–32; complexities of, 33–35; initial reception of, 34; criticisms of, 35–37, 39–41; as expression of its times, 42. *See also* Watson, Thomas E.; Populism
Turkey, 123
Turner, Frederick Jackson, 6, 127

157

Index